Challenging church

1 CORINTHIANS 1 – 9

by Mark Dever

thegoodbook
COMPANY

Challenging church
the good book guide to 1 corinthians
This US co-edition published with 9Marks 2012
Reprinted 2014
© Mark Dever/The Good Book Company, 2012.

To learn more about 9Marks and order
more material, visit www.9Marks.org

IX 9Marks
Building Healthy Churches

The Good Book Company
Tel: (US): 866 244 2165
Tel (UK): 0345-225-0880
Tel (int): + (44) 208-942-0880
Email: info@thegoodbook.com

Websites
N America: www.thegoodbook.com
UK: www.thegoodbook.co.uk
Australia: www.thegoodbook.com.au
New Zealand: www.thegoodbook.co.nz

thegoodbook
COMPANY

ISBN: 9781908317681

Printed in the Czech Republic

CONTENTS

introduction: good book guides

Every Bible-study group is different—yours may take place in a church building, in a home or in a cafe, on a train, over a leisurely mid-morning coffee or squashed into a 30-minute lunch break. Your group may include new Christians, mature Christians, non-Christians, moms and tots, students, businessmen or teens. That's why we've designed these *Good Book Guides* to be flexible for use in many different situations.

Our aim in each session is to uncover the meaning of a passage, and see how it fits into the "big picture" of the Bible. But that can never be the end. We also need to appropriately apply what we have discovered to our lives. Let's take a look at what is included:

⊕ **Talkabout:** Most groups need to "break the ice" at the beginning of a session, and here's the question that will do that. It's designed to get people talking around a subject that will be covered in the course of the Bible study.

⊥ **Investigate:** The Bible text for each session is broken up into manageable chunks, with questions that aim to help you understand what the passage is about. **The Leader's Guide** contains **guidance on questions**, and sometimes ☺ additional "follow-up" questions.

⊡ **Explore more (optional):** These questions will help you connect what you have learned to other parts of the Bible, so you can begin to fit it all together like a jig-saw; or occasionally look at a part of the passage that's not dealt with in detail in the main study.

→ **Apply:** As you go through a Bible study, you'll keep coming across **apply** sections. These are questions to get the group discussing what the Bible teaching means in practice for you and your church. ☺ **Getting personal** is an opportunity for you to think, plan and pray about the changes that you personally may need to make as a result of what you have learned.

↑ **Pray:** We want to encourage prayer that is rooted in God's word—in line with His concerns, purposes and promises. So each session ends with an opportunity to review the truths and challenges highlighted by the Bible study, and turn them into prayers of request and thanksgiving.

The **Leader's Guide** and introduction provide historical background information, explanations of the Bible texts for each session, ideas for **optional extra** activities, and guidance on how best to help people uncover the truths of God's word.

why study 1 Corinthians?

Even today, Jesus is still a figure of intense interest and admiration for millions. His stories and sayings still inhabit our minds 2000 years after He lived, and to many there is something compellingly beautiful about Him.

But then there's the church. If you've grown up in a church, you've probably got some good reasons to be disillusioned with it. The church seems like a boring topic for most, and a reluctantly fulfilled duty for many. If you introduce the subject, you'll often find it meets with responses ranging from a mild disinterest to a real dislike.

And we can understand why. Churches say they have the best news in the world, that they have the answer to our problems, that they are God's embassies on earth; and yet churches are made up of people like you and me, who are grumpy, irritable, unfaithful, selfish, and worse. Too possessive of small things and too casual about great ones. Too defensive of our interests and too often ignoring God.

And as that is sadly true of churches today, so it was of the church God had set up in Corinth through the apostle Paul. It was young, it was full of life, and it was just as full of problems. We see no single congregation in the New Testament in which there were more issues, and of such differing kinds. What would God say to such a challenging church? What did they need to be excited by, to listen to, to learn?

This Good Book Guide will help you to open up the first nine chapters of the letter of 1 Corinthians. It is a long, varied and often complex book. These studies are not a hike through every small detail, but more of a helicopter ride enabling you to see its peaks, as you hear what God said to His church in Corinth, and what God still says to His church today.

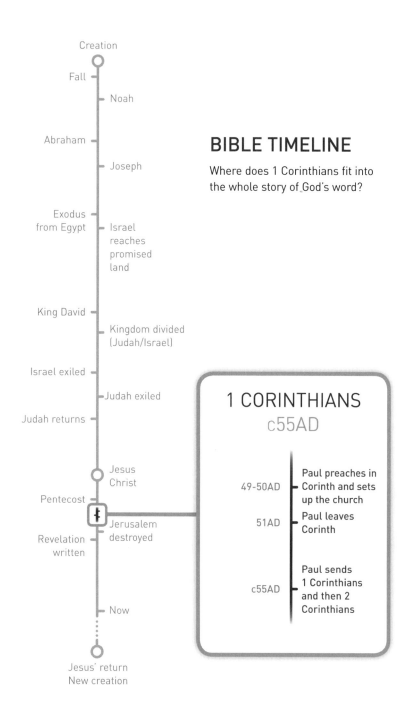

Creation

Fall

Noah

Abraham

Joseph

Exodus
from Egypt

Israel
reaches
promised
land

King David

Kingdom divided
(Judah/Israel)

Israel exiled

Judah exiled

Judah returns

Jesus
Christ

Pentecost

Jerusalem
destroyed

Revelation
written

Now

Jesus' return
New creation

BIBLE TIMELINE

Where does 1 Corinthians fit into
the whole story of God's word?

1 CORINTHIANS
c55AD

49-50AD	Paul preaches in Corinth and sets up the church
51AD	Paul leaves Corinth
c55AD	Paul sends 1 Corinthians and then 2 Corinthians

1

1 Corinthians 1 v 1-9

COUNT YOUR BLESSINGS

⊕ talkabout

1. How forgetful are you, and what sort of things do you tend to forget?

- Have you ever forgotten something which led to a comedy moment? Or a serious problem?

⊕ investigate

> **Read 1 Corinthians 1 v 1-9**

2. Who is this letter from and to?

> **DICTIONARY**
>
> **Apostle (v 1):** someone chosen and sent by Jesus to teach and serve the Christian church.
> **Sosthenes (v 1):** possibly a former Jewish leader (see Acts 18 v 17). Now one of Paul's co-workers.
> **Sanctified (v 2):** made clean and pure.
> **Holy (v 2):** set apart; totally pure.
> **Grace (v 3,4):** undeserved kindness.

God had used Paul to establish the church in Corinth in Greece during his second "missionary journey", in about 50-51AD (you can read about it in Acts 18). It was a few years later, probably between 52 and 55AD, that Paul wrote this letter to the church God had planted through him.

Corinth was a major crossroads between the eastern and western parts of the Roman Empire. A great trading centre, with people moving in and out all the time, it had a reputation for immorality and for its many religions. In other words, its society was much like many today.

3. Turn forward to these verses later on in the letter to see what this church was like:

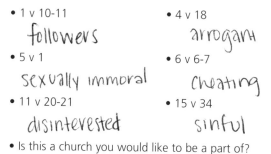

- 1 v 10-11

  followers

- 5 v 1

  sexually immoral

- 11 v 20-21

  disinterested

- 4 v 18

  arrogant

- 6 v 6-7

  cheating

- 15 v 34

  sinful

- Is this a church you would like to be a part of?

4. Back in chapter 1, pick out the ways Paul describes what has happened to these Corinthians, and fill in the first blank column in the table below:

	What?	How?
v 2	holy	Jesus
v 4	grace given	Jesus
v 5	enriched	Jesus
v 9	called	

Paul is helping them to recall the riches of God's blessing of Jesus. And did you notice that in verse 2, these Christians are described as already "sanctified (set apart as pure) in Christ Jesus"; but they are also "called" to be holy (to *become* set apart as pure). So are they set apart, or not?!

God has declared Christians to be set apart in right relationship with Him, because Christ's holiness and righteousness has been accounted, or freely given, to them. A Christian's status is "holy". But they are also called to *become* holy, to have lives which more fully reflect God's character, lives like they were meant to have. Having been made holy in Christ, they are now to live more and more as the people He has made them to be, living in accordance with their status as holy people.

5. What is the church looking forward to?

6. What will they be on that day? Why can they be confident they will still be Christians then?

7. Why is verse 7 an encouraging reminder for a church, particularly if it is small or struggling?

☺ getting personal

Do you ever think to yourself that you could do this, or that, as a Christian, if only you had been given this gift (better memory, sense of humor, teaching ability) or that circumstance (more time, greater wealth, different family, bigger church)?

Verse 7 says there is **no** spiritual gift you lack as a church. In which area do you need to stop making excuses and get on with living and working for God? Or do you need to stop thinking you can do everything yourself, and remember that you need to use your gifts for your church, and rely on others in your church to use their gifts to help and encourage you?

8. Who has blessed, or gifted, these Corinthians in this way? What are we told about His character in verse 9, and why is this important?

9. What does Paul tell his readers he is doing in verse 4?

10. Think about what the Corinthian church was like. What is surprising about verse 4?

• Why do you think Paul began his letter by talking about what God had given them?

11. Go back to the table on page 8. For each of those verses, fill in "How" it is that God gives His church each of the blessings you've listed in the "What" column.

⊟ apply

12. What do you think Paul wanted the Corinthians to do as they read these verses? What would he want us to do today?

13. How can we imitate Paul:

• in our prayers?

• as we speak to our Christian friends?

14. Look at the table on page 8. Which blessing has particularly struck you?

• How can you make sure you call God's generosity to mind regularly through the course of each day?

⊡ getting personal

Have you forgotten how much you have been given by God in Christ? Do you tend to focus on what you haven't been given in life, rather than on what you have?

Which blessing from God could you give thanks for each day for a month?

Who can you share that blessing with this week?

⊡ pray

• For other Christians, based on verse 4.

• For your church, based on verse 7.

• For yourself, giving thanks for a particular blessing you've been reminded of in this passage.

• For people, situations and issues which are on your group's hearts at the moment.

2

1 Corinthians 1 v 10 – 2 v 16
UNITE IN "FOOLISHNESS"

The story so far

As Paul has written to the Corinthian church, he has reminded them they've been given great gifts by God in Christ. God's given them all they need to keep going to eternal life.

⊕ talkabout

1. What opinions do people listen to about how to live? What is it that makes us listen to particular people's opinions?

⊕ investigate

> **Read 1 Corinthians 1 v 10-17**

2. What problem in the church is mentioned here (v 10-12)?

• What does Paul want them to do about it?

What is going on in the culture around a church often affects what goes on inside it. This young church in Corinth was no different. It was full of people who were used to hearing professional speakers on the streets of Corinth, speakers who gained a reputation more by their method of speech than what they said. People committed to and championed the speaker they felt sounded most impressive; and in doing so sought to look impressive themselves.

This was the context these Christians lived and breathed in, and this was the way they were viewing their own leaders within the church.

⊡ apply

3. When does respect for a Christian leader become unhealthy?

⊡ investigate

▶ **Read 1 Corinthians 1 v 18-31**

4. What are the two reactions to the message of the cross (v 18)?

5. Will the Christian message ever sound impressive to the world? Why, or why not?

6. What can human wisdom never do?

⊟ ## apply

7. What is "the message of the cross"? Why does it appear foolish to people today?

• So what will often happen when we tell people about Jesus? How is this a challenge to us?

⊔ investigate

8. Had these Christians chosen God, or had He chosen them (v 26-28)?

9. How impressive are these people by "human standards"? Why has God made the church like this?

10. Christian leaders will not sound impressive. Christian churches will not look impressive. Who are Christians to see as "impressive" (v 30-31)?

11. If the whole church does as Paul tells them to in verse 31, why would that stop them being divided and help them stay united?

> **Read 1 Corinthians 2 v 1-5**

12. How was Paul different to the spectacular, impressive-sounding speakers in Corinth?

13. What did Paul think was most important about his ministry (v 2)?

14. An unimpressive man, with an unimpressive message, delivered in an unimpressive way—why did Paul's words have any effect at all?

⊡ apply

15. Imagine you found yourself moving to another community and looking for a new church. What should you look for most of all?

⊡ explore more

▶ Read 1 Corinthians 2 v 6-16

Where does true wisdom come from, and what is it like (v 6-8)?

How do we get this type of wisdom?

⊡ getting personal

Do you ignore God's wisdom if the world says it is foolish?

Do you find yourself listening to the world's wisdom even when you know God says it's foolish?

How much of your day do you spend listening to the world, and how much listening to God in His word? If this needs to change, what will you do about it?

⬆ pray

Thank God...

for choosing you to be part of His people.

Pray for your church...

that it would be united around the message of the cross.

Pray for yourself...

about what has most struck you personally from this passage.

3 1 Corinthians 3
UNITE AS GOD'S COMMUNITY

The story so far

As Paul has written to the Corinthian church, he has:

- reminded them they've been given great gifts by God in Christ. God's given them all they need to keep going to eternal life.
- urged them to be united around the "foolish" message of Christ's cross, instead of being divided.

⊕ talkabout

1. Describe in one sentence what you think "church" is.

⊥ investigate

> Read 1 Corinthians 3 v 1-9

2. How does Paul describe these Christians (v 1)?

> **DICTIONARY**
>
> **Apollos (v 4,5,6):** a Christian leader who had been preaching in Corinth shortly after Paul left the city (see Acts 18 v 24-28).

3. What are the visible signs of this (v 3-4)?

4. In verses 5-9, how does Paul describe:

 • God?

 • himself, Apollos and any other Christian worker?

5. Who should Christians say they follow?

⊡ apply

6. How would you encourage someone who said to you: *"I've given up telling people about Jesus. It just never seems to work. I'll never make anyone a Christian"*?

Think for a moment about what in your life is:
• helping you to grow up as a Christian.
• hindering your growth.
What are you going to change?

⊕ investigate

❯ Read 1 Corinthians 3 v 10-23

DICTIONARY

Grace (v 10):
undeserved kindness.
The Day (v 13):
the future day Jesus
returns to the world
in power.
Futile (v 20):
pointless.

7. As Paul looks forward to "the Day" that Jesus is revealed (1 v 7), what does he say will happen at that time?

• v 12-13

• v 14-15

In the Old Testament, the temple in Jerusalem was the place where God chose to make His dwelling, where He is most present on earth.

8. What is exciting about what Paul says in verse 16? Why is it a motivation to stay united?

In verse 21 Paul says "no more boasting about human leaders!". Paul wants the Corinthians to stop giving allegiance to the Christian leader they find most impressive. He wants them to stop boasting about their relationship with a particular leader.

9. How have verses 5-17 shown the foolishness of doing this?

10. In verses 21-23, what does Paul say these Christians have?

11. What three warnings does Paul give them in this section?

- v 10, 13

- v 17

- v 18

12. What three things is Paul telling us about God's relationship to the church?

- v 6-9

- v 10

- v 16

⊡ **getting personal**

Are you growing as a Christian? Why / why not?

Have you realized that your church belongs to God, not you; and His wishes and plans for it are more important than your preferences?

Is there any part of your attitude towards church which you need to change?

⊟ **apply**

13. Using this passage, how would you respond to a friend who said:

- *"I really only like to listen to (insert name of preacher); he's just so much more inspiring and interesting than any other speaker I've heard"*?

- *"We spend too much time thinking about what church should be like: we need just to get out there and tell people about Christ"?*

⬆ pray

Write down three prayer points, based on this passage.

-

-

-

4 RECOGNIZE REAL MINISTERS

The story so far

As Paul has written to the Corinthian church, he has:

- reminded them they've been given great gifts by God in Christ. God's given them all they need to keep going to eternal life.

- urged them to be united around the "foolish" message of Christ's cross, instead of being divided.

- explained that the church is built on the foundation of Christ, dwelled in by the Spirit, and grown by God.

⊕ talkabout

1. What makes a good church minister? What should their priorities be?

⊕ investigate

How can you recognize the real from the fake? Paul knew that some leaders in the Corinthian church were imposters. The gospel had been silenced by their substitute message. They were "arrogant" (4 v 18-19), thinking they knew better than God's own apostle, Paul. They relied not on God's power but on their own words (4 v 20). And they were leading people away from Christ.

So how could these young Christians recognize the real from the fake? Paul gives three key qualities of a real Christian minister or pastor, which we will pick out as we look through chapter 4.

Key Quality One

> **Read 1 Corinthians 4 v 1-7**

2. What do those who have been entrusted with church leadership need to do (v 2)?

3. Whose judgements does Paul not care about (v 3)?

-
-
-

4. Whose judgment *does* Paul care about, and when will this judgment happen (v 5)?

5. Paul has said ministers must be "faithful"; and verse 6 tells us some of what it means to be faithful. What should Paul, Apollos and any other church leader *not* do?

6. Paul summed up the content of God's message in 2 v 2. What is it?

⊡ **apply**

7. Why might it be tempting for a church minister to "go beyond what is written" (4 v 6)?

8. How can we help our pastors make sure they don't do this?

A real minister preaches a cross-centered message.

⊡ **getting personal**

Do you know the freedom of knowing that:
• the only judgment that matters is God's?
• if you are a Christian, then because of His Son's death God has forgiven you and sees you as perfect?
Or do you care more and worry more about the judgments of others?

You cannot please God if you live to please men. And you are unlikely to please men if you live to please God. What difference does this truth make to your life and ambitions?

Whose judgment do *you* care more about: that of your friends, family, church and work colleagues, or your Lord and Savior's?

⬇ investigate

Key Quality Two

▶ **Read 1 Corinthians 4 v 8-13**

9. Pick out how Paul describes:

The Corinthians' view of themselves	Paul's view of himself
rich strong wise honored kings	condemned fools weak dishonored poor abused spectacle

10. It appears the fake teachers had been promising the Corinthians wealth and power. How does Paul's life show that these are false promises?

11. Paul describes his experience of real Christian ministry. Read **Luke 9 v 58** and **1 Peter 2 v 21-24**. How is minister Paul's experience similar to that of his Master—Jesus Christ?

A real minister lives a cross-centered life.

Key Quality Three

> **Read 1 Corinthians 4 v 14-21**

12. How does Paul describe his relationship with the Corinthians? Why does he think of himself in this way?

13. Paul lives a cross-centered life. What kind of life does he want the Christians in his care to have (v 16)?

A real minister encourages cross-centered followers.

Paul says he's sending Timothy, a real, "faithful" pastor, to them. Have a look at verse 17 to see what Timothy's going to remind them of:

- "my way of life in Christ Jesus" = Paul's cross-centered life

- "which agrees with what I teach" = Paul's cross-centered message

→ **apply**

14. Based on this passage, how would you respond to these two situations?

- After the church service, a member of your small group is annoyed with the minister. *"I can't believe he said that sex outside marriage is wrong,"* she says. *"I mean, life's more complicated than that, isn't it? And I've got a friend visiting who doesn't come to church much; what's he going to think? Why can't the pastor tone it down a bit?"*

- A friend from church has bought a brand new sports car. *"I wasn't sure about getting it, but then I realized God would want me to buy it,"* he tells you. *"God has given us all good things as part of His promise to us in the gospel, hasn't He? It's right that His people enjoy the wealth He has given us."*

optional

⊡ explore more

When Paul revisits Corinth, what are the two options for how he treats these Christians (v 21)?

The way in which the believers prepare for his coming will determine the nature of Paul's visit. He's like a loving father who longs to be gentle, but who for the sake of his children's integrity is prepared to be tough. This is a good reminder that both gentleness and severity are part of Christian love and leadership.

⊡ getting personal

Are there areas of your life which you'd rather your pastor didn't preach from the Bible about?

Imagine… As they are preaching, your minister shows you from the Bible an area of your life where you are self-centered, not cross-centered. How will you react? What should you think to yourself? What should you say to your minister?

↑ pray

Together…

How can you give thanks for, and pray for, your church's minister(s) from what God's Spirit has said in this Bible section?

Alone…

What aspect of what you've seen do you need to ask for God's help with?

5

1 Corinthians 5 – 6
DON'T GO SOFT ON SIN

The story so far

As Paul has written to the Corinthian church, he has:

- urged them to be united around the "foolish" message of Christ's cross, instead of being divided.
- explained that the church is built on the foundation of Christ, dwelled in by the Spirit, and grown by God.
- told them real Christian ministers are cross-centered in their message, in how they live, and in how they encourage others to live.

⊕ talkabout

1. *"It's not right to judge what anyone else does."* Do you agree or disagree? Are there any situations in which you'd change your answer?

⊕ investigate

▶ **Read 1 Corinthians 5 v 1-5**

2. What has Paul heard has happened in this church?

DICTIONARY

Pagans (v 1): people who don't know the real God.

• How have the other church members reacted (v 2)?

3. What should they be doing?

Paul wants them to "hand this man over to Satan" (v 5): that is, the public removal of the church's affirmation that he's saved.

4. What does he hope this will result in (end of v 5)? What is the aim of biblical church discipline?

5. Read **Matthew 18 v 15-17**. How are Paul's commands to this church reflecting Jesus' teaching during His time on earth?

> **Read 1 Corinthians 5 v 6-8**

Paul pictures this man's sin as "yeast" in the "dough" of the Corinthian church.

6. If it's not dealt with, what will happen (v 6)?

The man's sin was a single serious infection, but the church's lack of discipline was a complete failure of the immune system. Sin that no one deals with becomes sin that everyone will have to deal with.

⊡ explore more

optional

How does Paul refer to Christ in verse 7?

Paul's referring to the exodus. We pick up the story as Moses is speaking to God's people, who are slaves in Egypt, about how God is going to rescue them.

> **Read Exodus 12 v 17-28**

What did the blood of the Passover lamb achieve for God's people in Egypt?

In the feast at which God's people showed their thanks for the exodus, yeast was significant. Why (v 17-20)?

How should Christians, who Christ died for, show they are part of His people today (1 Corinthians 5 v 8)?

➔ apply

7. Many Christians instinctively don't want to think about discipline or confront public sin. Why do you think this is?

• If there were no discipline in your church, what might the result be?

getting personal

If God declares something is sinful, we must not cultivate an indifference to it, regardless of cultural acceptance of the issue. We want to love God so much that we hate the sin that He hates, both in ourselves and in others.

Do you truly grieve when people at your church stop trusting in Christ, leave the church and live without Him?

Is there a Christian you know who needs you to help them by confronting them about a particular repeated and public sin?

⊙ **investigate**

❱ **Read 1 Corinthians 5 v 9-12**

8.   Paul reminds his readers "not to associate with sexually immoral people" (v 9). What *doesn't* he mean by this (v 10)?

Idolaters (v 10): people who most love and worship something other than God.
Brother or sister (v 11): another Christian.
Slanderer (v 11): someone who tries to ruin people's reputations by saying untrue things about them.
Swindler (v 11): someone who cheats people out of their money or possessions.

• What *does* he mean (v 11)?

Paul goes on to talk about who Christians should judge. He quotes God's words to Old Testament Israel: "Expel the wicked man from among you" (Deuteronomy 17 v 7). And he applies this to the New Testament church.

9.   Whose business *isn't* it for the church to judge (v 12)? Who will do this?

- Whose business *is* it for the Christian community to judge?

- But the church is often tempted to judge the world while refusing to judge itself. Why do you think this is?

To refuse to judge sin in the church is to obscure the gospel. That means that we end up harming ourselves, especially the weakest and most vulnerable among us—those who are trapped in their sin.

optional

⊡ explore more

▶ **Read 1 Corinthians 6 v 1-8**

What has been going on in the Corinthian church (v 1, 6)?

These people clearly want to get what they feel they deserve—even if it means going to court.

What attitude does Paul recommend instead (v 7)?

▶ **Read Philippians 2 v 5-11**

What will inspire Christians to give up what they deserve, instead of insisting on it?

▶ **Read 1 Corinthians 6 v 9-11**

10. Why does sin matter so much (v 9-10)?

DICTIONARY
Sanctified (v 11): set apart to live for God, by living like God.
Justified (v 11): found "not guilty" of something and declared completely innocent.

- If a church does not discipline people who live like that, they might be "deceived" (v 9) into thinking it's fine. Why does this matter?

- What is the great news Paul reminds us about?

- Why does Paul repeat the word "were" in verse 11, do you think?

▶ Read 1 Corinthians 6 v 12-20

The church seems to have got the idea that what they do with their physical bodies doesn't really matter (v 12-13). So sexual immorality isn't really that serious.

11. Paul gives four reasons why sexual immorality really *does* matter. Each one is a really exciting truth about God! Pick them out:

	Truth about God	Why it shows sexual immorality matters
v 14		
v 15-16		
v 18-19a		
v 19b-20		

getting personal

God cares about what you do with your body. A moral and right use of the body honors God. Sin will always be part of a Christian's life: but unrepentant sin must cease.

Are you struggling with sexual sin? Have you admitted it to yourself and to God, and asked Him to wash you and forgive you?

When you are next tempted to sin in this way, what truth about God do you need to remember?

➔ apply

12. *"It's not right to judge people."* What would Paul say to your church about this attitude?

• What part must each individual church member play in keeping their church pure?

⬆ pray

Thank God...

• for the great truths of 1 Corinthians 6 v 11.

Ask God...

• to help you to help your church community by taking sin seriously.

• to give your church courage when difficult decisions need to be taken.

• to help you personally with a sin you're particularly struggling with.

6

1 Corinthians 7
LET YOUR CALLING COUNT

The story so far

As Paul has written to the Corinthian church, he has:

- explained that the church is built on the foundation of Christ, dwelled in by the Spirit, and grown by God.
- told them real Christian ministers are cross-centered in their message, how they live, and how they encourage others to live.
- warned them not to be complacent about sin in the church, but to lovingly and humbly expose and discipline those who are sinning.

⊕ talkabout

1. If you surveyed 100 people in your area, asking them what they needed to make them happy, what would the most popular answers be?

⊕ investigate

This chapter is about sex, marriage and singleness. But before looking at Paul's instructions to the Corinthian Christians (and us) on these specific issues, let's grapple with some general principles Paul gives them (and us)...

> **Read 1 Corinthians 7 v 17-31**

DICTIONARY
Circumcised (v 18-19): in Old Testament times, God told His people to show they were trusting in His promises by being circumcised (if they were men).

2. What is the idea Paul repeats most often in verses 17-24?

- Paul's using this repetition to make a point. There's something more important about our identity than our circumstances (circumcised or uncircumcised, slave or free). What is it?

3. In v 22, what does Paul call slaves? What does he call those who are free?

- What point do you think he is making?

4. Why is being "called" by God more important than our circumstances?
- v 29

- v 31

⊡ apply

5. Think back to Question One. What types of circumstances are those around us working hard to gain, or to keep?

• Why will the answers to Question Four enable us to have a different perspective?

6. The bulk of this chapter (which we'll look at next) is about marriage, sex and singleness. As we approach these difficult, emotional issues, why are the truths we've seen vital to keep in mind?

⊡ getting personal

Do you want to change your circumstances, or serve Christ through them?

Do you need to pray more about living for God, and less about Him changing your situation?

Do you see dark days as an opportunity to serve Christ, rather than an excuse not to?

⬇ investigate

❯ Read 1 Corinthians 7 v 1-16

In verse 1, Paul is probably quoting from what the Corinthian church "wrote about" in a letter to him. It seems some of them thought sex and marriage were somehow unspiritual and worldly, and not right for Christians who are looking forward to Jesus' return.

7. What answer does Paul give (v 1-5)?

• What reasons does Paul give for getting married (v 2, 4)?

8. Having dealt with the issue of beginning a marriage, Paul turns to the issue of the ending of marriages. Complete the table to see how he says Christians should deal with different situations.

	Situation	Command
v 10-11		
v 12-14		
v 15-16		
v 39-40		

In verse 10, Paul points out that his advice is based on a command Jesus gave while on earth.

❯ **Read Matthew 19 v 1-12**

What does Jesus teach about divorce in verses 4-6, and why?

So, why does the law God gave to Moses accept the existence of divorce (v 8)?

Under what circumstances does Jesus say divorce is allowed (v 9)?

How does the disciples' reaction in verse 10 mirror Paul's words in 1 Corinthians 7 v 28?!

⊖ **apply**

9. We've seen a Christian view of sex, marriage and divorce. How is this different to the view of the society in which you live?

• How does Paul's teaching guard us against making:

too much of marriage?

too little of marriage?

⊥ investigate

Not everyone is married. Not everyone will get married. Paul himself was a single man, and in verse 7 he calls singleness a "gift", just as marriage is. Some are gifted with a spouse: others are gifted with singleness. Both are given as a good gift from God!

❯ Read 1 Corinthians 7 v 32-35

10. What does Paul say are the advantages of being single?

• What do these verses add to Paul's view of singleness?

v 26, v 29-31

v 28

⊡ apply

11. What does society see as the advantages and disadvantages of singleness?

• How is this the same and/or different to how the Bible sees it?

12. Imagine you have a Christian friend who is married to someone who isn't a Christian. Their faith has caused problems in their marriage, and they're wondering what to do. What advice would you give them, based on 1 Corinthians 7?

• Imagine you have a Christian friend who is single and would rather not be. How would you encourage them from these verses?

☺ getting personal

If you are married, are you loving your spouse by treating everything you have as belonging to them (v 4)? How could you do this more?

If you are single, are you using the extra time and emotional energy that you have to "live in a right way in undivided devotion to the Lord" (v 35)? Are there any changes you need to make to do this more?

Would it help to say to yourself each morning: "I have been called by God to be a child of God. That is the most important thing about who I am, and serving Him in the circumstances He's given me is the most satisfying thing I can do with my day."

⊡ pray

Thank God for...

- making you His child.

- giving you the circumstances you are in.

Ask God to...

- help you be satisfied with the circumstances He has gifted you (you might like to share with the rest of the group any particular areas of your life in which you need God's help to do this).

- remind you that you can serve Him whatever your situation, feelings and relationships.

7

1 Corinthians 8 – 9

USE YOUR RIGHTS

The story so far

As Paul has written to the Corinthian church, he has:

- told them real Christian ministers are cross-centered in their message, in how they live, and in how they encourage others to live.
- warned them not to be complacent about sin in the church, but to lovingly and humbly expose and discipline those who are sinning.
- encouraged them to use their circumstances to serve God, whether they're single, married or widowed.

talkabout

1. What are your most important rights? Would you ever give them up, or allow them to be taken from you?

investigate

Read 1 Corinthians 8 v 1-13

Paul says Christians "all possess knowledge" (v 1): they all know and understand the gospel message.

DICTIONARY

Idols (v 1,4,7,10): things people worship, serve and trust instead of the real God.
Weak (v 7,10,12): here, it means untaught, or unknowing.
Conscience (v 7,10,12): our internal guide to what is right and wrong.
Emboldened (v 10): given courage to do something.

2. Why do we need love as well as knowledge (v 1)?

Paul is talking about the practice of eating food sacrificed to idols (v 4); but he's also setting out a principle that applies in all areas of life.

Animal sacrifices were a regular part of ancient pagan worship. The temple served as not only a place of worship but also as a butcher's shop. People served meat that had originated as a sacrifice in the pagan temple.

3. What do Christians know about God (v 4, 6)?

• What does this mean about other gods that people worship (v 5-6)?

4. What does Paul therefore say all Christians should *know* (v 8)?

• So, does it matter whether or not Christians eat meat that has been used in idol worship?

5. Paul knows that some of the Corinthian Christians don't know that eating meat used in idol worship is fine. What's the problem if they eat such meat (v 7, 10-11)?

6. What point is Paul making to Christians who know it's fine to eat this meat (v 9, 13)?

• What is the *loving* thing for *knowledgeable* Christians to do?

• What point does Paul make in verse 12?

⮕ apply

7. What principle is Paul establishing as he talks about whether to eat meat sacrificed to idols?

8. Simon is buying a brand new car to replace his two-year old model. As he tells Warren about it after the church service, he encourages him to do the same. Warren replies that he thinks it's wrong for a Christian to replace their car when there's no need to. They both quickly change the subject!

• What should Simon be asking himself after talking to Warren?

• What should Warren be asking himself after talking to Simon?

• In what other situations today do Christians need to be careful that our freedom "does not become a stumbling block"?

The bottom line is this: we learn obedience by good teaching, and knowledge should be guided by love.

🙂 getting personal

Are you growing in knowledge of how to obey God by educating your conscience from God's word as much as you can?

Are you motivated by love for fellow Christians when you know more than a brother or sister about how to live?

In what way is *your* knowledge—or how you live because of your knowledge—in danger of harming other Christians?

⊡ investigate

❯ Read 1 Corinthians 9 v 1-23

In verses 1-3, Paul reminds us that he is free because he is a Christian: and also that he is an apostle (v 1), who is therefore a model to other believers.

DICTIONARY

Apostle (v 1,2,5): someone chosen by God to serve and teach the Christian church.
Seal (v 2): a mark showing something was authentic, not a fake (often used on letters or documents).
Compelled (v 16): forced.
Discharging (v 17): doing all that is needed to perform a duty.

9. What does Paul say he is free to do as an apostle?

• v 4

• v 5

• v 9-12, 14

10. What has Paul decided to do with the rights he enjoys as a Christian and as an apostle (v 12, 15, 19)?

• Why (v 19-22)?

11. Think back over what you've seen this Corinthian church was like from chapters 1 to 9. What were their priorities?

• How would verse 19 have been a real challenge to them?

⊡ **explore more**

❯ **Read 1 Corinthians 9 v 24-27**

Paul compares the Christian to a runner, focused on reaching the finish line (v 24); and to a boxer, ensuring every action counts (v 26).

What does this look like for him (v 27)?

How does this encourage any Christians who teach others? And what's the warning?

⊡ **apply**

12. What rights do we find hardest to be willing to give up?

• How will 8 v 9 and 9 v 19 motivate us to give up the freedoms we hold most dear?

⊡ **getting personal**

What rights do you struggle to be willing to give up for the sake of others? Your weekends, or Sunday evenings? Time with your friends? A particular kind of music? Your home country or large house? Your desire to do what you want, when you want? Your holidays?

Would it be worth memorizing 9 v 19: "Though I am free and belong to no one, I have made myself a slave to everyone, to win as many as possible".

⬆ **pray**

Thank God for...

Pray for your group...

Pray for those around you who aren't yet sharing in the gospel's blessings...

Challenging church

1 Corinthians

LEADER'S GUIDE

Leader's Guide: Introduction

INTRODUCTION

Leading a Bible study can be a bit like herding cats—everyone has a different idea of what the passage could be about, and a different line of enquiry that they want to pursue. But a good group leader is more than someone who just referees this kind of discussion. You will want to:

- correctly understand and handle the Bible passage. But also…

- encourage and train the people in your group to do this for themselves. Don't fall into the trap of spoon-feeding people by simply passing on the information in the Leader's Guide. Then…

- make sure that no Bible study is finished without everyone knowing how the passage is relevant for them. What changes do you all need to make in the light of the things you have been learning? And finally…

- encourage the group to turn all that has been learned and discussed into prayer.

Your Bible-study group is unique, and you are likely to know better than anyone the capabilities, backgrounds and circumstances of the people you are leading. That's why we've designed these guides with a number of optional features. If they're a quiet bunch, you might want to spend longer on talkabout. If your time is limited, you can choose to skip explore more, or get people to look at these questions at home. And each study has an optional extra section, which helps introduce or reinforce a theme of the passage. As leader, you can adapt and select the material to the needs of your particular group.

So what's in the Leader's Guide? The main thing that this Leader's Guide will help you to do is to understand the major teaching points in the passage you are studying, and how to apply them. As well as guidance on the questions, the Leader's Guide for each session contains the following important sections:

THE BIG IDEA

One key sentence will give you the main point of the session. This is what you should be aiming to have fixed in people's minds as they leave the Bible study. And it's the point you need to head back towards when the discussion goes off at a tangent.

SUMMARY

An overview of the passage, including plenty of useful historical background information.

OPTIONAL EXTRA

Usually this is an introductory activity that ties in with the main theme of the Bible study, and is designed to "break the ice" at the start of a session. Or it may be a way of illustrating a complex or important point, or reinforcing and extending an application towards the end of the session.

So let's take a look at the various different features of a Good Book Guide:

⊕ talkabout

Each session kicks off with a discussion question, based on the group's opinions or experiences. It's designed to get people talking and thinking in a general way about the main subject of the Bible study.

⊕ investigate

The first thing you and your group need to know is what the Bible passage is about, which is the purpose of these questions. But watch out—people may come up with answers based on their experiences or teaching they have heard in the past, without referring to the passage at all. It's amazing how often we can get through a Bible study without actually looking at the Bible! If you're stuck for an answer, the Leader's Guide contains guidance on questions. These are the answers to direct your group to. This information isn't meant to be read out to people—ideally, you want them to discover these answers from the Bible for themselves. Sometimes there are optional follow-up questions (see ⊗ in guidance on questions) to help you help your group get to the answer.

⊡ explore more

These questions generally point people to other relevant parts of the Bible. They are useful for helping your group to see how the passage fits into the "big picture" of the whole Bible. These sections are OPTIONAL—only use them if you have time. Remember that it's better to finish in good time having really grasped one big thing from the passage, than to try to cram everything in.

⊖ apply

We want to encourage you to spend more time working at application—too often, it is simply tacked on at the end. In the Good Book Guides, apply sections are mixed in with the investigate sections of the study. We hope that people will realise that application is not just an optional extra, but rather, the whole purpose of studying the

Bible. We do Bible study so that our lives can be changed by what we hear from God's word. If you skip the application, the Bible study hasn't achieved its purpose.

These questions draw out practical lessons that we can all learn from the Bible passage. You can review what has been learned so far, and think about practical differences that this should make in our churches and our lives. The group gets the opportunity to talk about what they personally have learned.

⊕ getting personal

These can be done at home, but it is well worth allowing a few moments of quiet reflection during the study for each person to think and pray about specific changes they need to make in their own lives. Why not have a time for reporting back at the beginning of the following session, so that everyone can be encouraged and challenged by one another to make application a priority?

⊕ pray

In Acts 4 v 25-30 the first Christians quoted Psalm 2 as they prayed in response to the persecution of the apostles by the Jewish religious leaders. Today however, it's not as common for Christians to base prayers on the truths of God's word as it once was. As a result, our prayers tend to be weak, superficial and self-centered rather than bold, visionary and God-centered.

The prayer section is based on what has been learned from the Bible passage. How different our prayer times would be if we were genuinely responding to what God has said to us through His word.

1

1 Corinthians 1 v 1-9

COUNT YOUR BLESSINGS

THE BIG IDEA

God has given Christians amazing blessings in Christ both now and for all eternity. We need to remember these blessings ourselves, and remind others of them.

SUMMARY

Paul usually tried to begin his letters with some kind of thanksgiving, but this was a church famous for its faults. We see no single church in the New Testament in which there were more problems, and of such differing kinds. We might think that if there were going to be a church Paul was not able to give thanks for, this would be it!

But in fact Paul does "thank ... God ... because of his grace given you in Christ Jesus" (v 4). And as he does so, he encourages them and us to look at all the riches Christians have; to look at all the blessings these Christians in Corinth knew, given to them by God and in Christ. There is a reason that Christians have sometimes been called simply "the blessed".

OPTIONAL EXTRA

Contact your group *before* you meet up for this opening study, and suggest they read through 1 Corinthians (either the whole book or chapters 1 – 9, which this Good Book Guide covers). This will allow people to see the general flow of the book before they study small parts in greater detail. Ask them to think about:

• the tone of the letter.
• the general themes of the letter.
• the challenges of the letter.
• what the letter tells us about the church in Corinth, and about their Lord, Jesus.

GUIDANCE ON QUESTIONS

1. How forgetful are you, and what sort of things do you tend to forget?
• **Have you ever forgotten something which led to a comedy moment? Or a serious problem?**
Get your group talking, and laughing, about forgetfulness. (If you have couples in the group, they may well remember each others' forgetfulness more than they do their own!) It would be helpful to have at least one recollection of a forgetful moment which caused a real problem—perhaps you could think of one to share yourself if necessary.

2. Who is this letter from and to? This is a letter written by Paul, an apostle (or "messenger") of Christ Jesus, chosen by God, and also from Sosthenes. He was clearly with Paul when this letter was written (probably in Ephesus); what is interesting about him is that he may well have been the Sosthenes mentioned in Acts 18 as God worked through Paul to establish this church in Corinth. When a frustrated mob was unable to have Paul successfully convicted and dealt with by Roman officials, we read in Acts 18 v 17 that they all "turned on Sosthenes the synagogue leader and beat him in front of the proconsul". At this stage he was a Jewish leader opposing Paul—but it appears from 1 Corinthians 1 v 1 that he was converted to Christ.
The letter is written to the Christian church in Corinth.

3. Turn forward to these verses later on in the letter to see what this church was like: The church God had founded in

Corinth was young, full of life, and just as full of problems. (You might like to divide your group into pairs and give them a couple of verses each to look at, to save some time, and then ask them briefly to tell the rest of the group what they saw.)

- **1 v 10-11:** Divisions and quarreling
- **4 v 18:** Arrogance
- **5 v 1:** Sexual immorality including sleeping with close relations
- **6 v 6-7:** Suing one another in court
- **11 v 20-21:** Getting drunk during the Lord's Supper meal
- **15 v 34:** Ignorance of God leading to sinful behavior

- **Is this a church you would like to be a part of?** Most of us would not want to join this church, with all its problems! This part of Q2 is to encourage your group to make a "value judgement" about this particular church, based on what the verses have shown them has been taking place within the congregation.

4. Back in chapter 1, pick out the ways Paul describes what has happened to these Corinthians, and fill in the first blank column in the table below: The table can be completed roughly like this (only complete the first column at this point: the How? column is for Q11):

	What?	**How?**
v 2	Sanctified, called to be holy	In (ie: united in relationship with) Christ Jesus
v 4	Given God's grace	In Christ Jesus
v 5	Given wonderful treasures in every way	In him (ie: Christ)

	What?	**How?**
v 9	Called into fellowship (ie: relationship) with Christ	n/a

The text below the table in the Study Guide deals with the "now-but-not-yet" nature of a Christian's holiness. We are holy (in and through Jesus)—but we need to become holy through living His way. You might like to use the illustration of a commoner who marries into a royal family. The moment she says "I will" to her prince, she becomes royalty, through union with him. But she also needs to behave as royalty, to live up to the status she now has. And she might find it takes a great deal of effort, and some time, before she is able to do that perfectly!

5. What is the church looking forward to? To Christ being "revealed" (v 7). You might like to ask the group what event Paul is thinking of when he talks of Christ being "revealed"; it is the day when He is able to be seen physically in all His glory on earth, what we usually tend to call His "return". As they looked toward that day, this church had an eager expectancy about them; they knew that, unlike our world's cruel counterfeits which promise so much but in the end deliver nothing, this would definitely come to pass.

6. What will they be on that day? Why can they be confident they will still be Christians then? The Corinthian church was full of people who were involved in various kinds of sin, but Paul assured them that on the day of Christ, there will be nothing to lay against the Christian; they will be blameless. Paul is not talking about *feeling* guilty, but *being* guilty before God—and it is this guilt Christians will be without on the final day of judgment (so they were able to eagerly wait for it, instead of dreading it).

They could know they would still be Christians on that day because God would strengthen them to keep them going until they made it there. Christians have been given the great gift of perseverance.

7. Why is verse 7 an encouraging reminder for a church, particularly if it is small or struggling? Verse 7 is greatly encouraging to any church, as it was meant to be for the Corinthian church. It tells us there is nothing God should have given us that He hasn't given us. We have all we need for what God has called us to do. The "you" in v 7 is plural, so Paul is not saying that each individual Christian has every gift from God, but that as a fellowship they have all they need.

⊻

- **APPLY: Some of the spiritual gifts we need have been given to other members of our church family: what does this mean we need to do as individual Christians?** We need to rely on one another and put our abilities at others' disposal, if as a church we are to serve God in all the ways He calls us to. (This question leads into the Getting Personal section after Q7.)

8. Who has blessed, or gifted, these Corinthians in this way? What are we told about His character in verse 9, and why is this important? It was God who had done all this for the Corinthians; all these blessings stand as tokens of God's own love. And God is faithful (in the Greek original, it is "faithful is God", as if to stress the point); Christians can have confidence

that they can trust God to keep delivering His promised help, each day and to the very end.

9. What does Paul tell his readers he is doing in verse 4? Paul thanks God for the Corinthian Christians—he knows that God is the source of all these blessings, that there is nothing good that Paul is seeing in the Corinthians that hasn't come from God Himself. Paul knew it was God who was behind the calling and blessing of these people.

10. Think about what the Corinthian church was like. What is surprising about verse 4? That Paul gives thanks at all for this church! If we were thinking in a worldly way, the *last* thing in the world we would do for such a church is to thank God for them! They had been full of problems, it seems, ever since their founding.

- **Why do you think Paul began his letter by talking about what God had given them?** Because he wants these Christians to remember the blessings God has given them.

⊻

- **What does Paul see as the most important thing about these people he's writing to?** That they had God's saving grace in their lives. Important as some of the sins of this congregation were—whether done through ignorance or, even worse, in defiance—they paled before what God had done for them. So Paul thanks God for them, and tells them he's thanking God for them.

**11. Go back to the table on page 8. For each of those verses, fill in "How" it is that God gives His church each of the blessings you've listed in the "What" column. See table previous page. Notice throughout these verses that God is pointing the Corinthians to the One through whom supremely He has blessed them—Christ.

EXPLORE MORE
Read Romans 8 v 31b-32. How are Christians able to know that God really will give them what they need to keep going in their faith? Because in giving us Christ, God has given us the best He could! If God has given us His only Son, He will give us everything that we need for life and godliness.

12. APPLY: What do you think Paul wanted the Corinthians to do as they read these verses? What would he want us to do today? Paul wanted the Corinthians to be encouraged in their faith and grateful to God for their blessings, to remind them of God's grace. The most important thing about them is that God has purchased them and His Spirit is at work in them. He wants the same for us.

13. APPLY: How can we imitate Paul:
• **in our prayers?** By giving thanks for our Christian brothers and sisters, even those who are struggling, who frustrate us, who are immature and unsteady in their Christian lives.

• **as we speak to our Christian friends?** By reminding our Christian friends about how blessed they are by God in Christ.

If time allows, refer back to Q1 and ask the group what effect it has when individual Christians or whole churches forget how God has blessed them.

14. APPLY: Look at the table on page 8. Which blessing has particularly struck

you? You might want to give your group time to write down an individual answer to this, and then ask people to share what they wrote down, and why. Then move on to think as a group about how you can regularly remember God's generosity.

• **How can you make sure you call God's generosity to mind regularly through the course of each day?** Ideas for how to call to mind the specific blessings of 1 Corinthians 1 v 1-9 during the day could include:
  • When you look in the mirror or see your reflection, remember that God sees you as pure, sanctified, because you are in Christ.
  • Whenever you spend money on something, remember that in Christ God has given you grace and spiritual gifts.
  • Whenever you look at your watch, remember that one day the Lord Jesus Christ will be revealed.
  • Whenever you see someone holding hands, remember that God will keep hold of you until Jesus returns.

Of course, your group may well have different and better ideas than these! More general possibilities include: texting one another; setting an alarm with a message on a laptop; sticking a verse on the desk at work or in a room at home.

2 1 Corinthians 1 v 10 – 2 v 16
UNITE IN "FOOLISHNESS"

THE BIG IDEA
Christians are to be united around the message of Christ's cross, even though this will look foolish and unimpressive to the world.

SUMMARY
It seems the Corinthian church had divided into people who followed different leaders, touting their loyalties to the various teachers as if they were peddlers selling their competing wares. Some claimed allegiance to Paul, some to Apollos, some to Cephas (possibly the apostle Peter) (v 12). The situation was an understandable one, since Corinth was a city full of eloquent speakers who won a following; and this was the context the church lived and breathed in.

Paul pointed out that the message is the important thing, not which book or friend or minister you may first hear it from. And the message is the cross of Christ (1 v 17, 18, 23, 2 v 2). The church was not to follow the world in following the person who seemed wisest, nor to expect the world to be impressed with the gospel message.

The message which Paul brought them was not impressive to the world, either in content or delivery (2 v 1-5), and the church itself was not full of impressive people; rather, God had deliberately chosen the unimpressive (1 v 26-29)!

GUIDANCE ON QUESTIONS
1. What opinions do people listen to about how to live? What is it that makes us listen to particular people's opinions? Possible sources for people's opinions include politicians, celebrities, radio

broadcasters, newspaper commentators, parents, friends, authors, DJs, ministers... and their popularity comes from different qualities. We listen to people's opinions for a variety of reasons:
- they are respectable.
- they have the life people want (such as celebrities).
- they are persuasive and good at putting their point across (writers in newspapers, politicians).
- they say what we already agree with or what we want to hear (newspapers, radio presenters, politicians!).

2. What problem in the church is mentioned here (v 10-12)? Some of the Christians in Corinth were being wrongly partisan and even divisive, by being loyal to one particular Christian teacher (who had baptized them) and sidelining all others. There can be a wrong attachment to ministers.

- **What does Paul want them to do about it?** Paul's basic command is to agree so that they will be perfectly united. This command and an exploration of the divisions that prevent unity takes Paul to the end of chapter 3 (the end of the next study).
Note: It may be that your group ask what exactly Christians need to agree on? Paul does not answer that question in this verse, but through the passage it becomes clear that Christians need to agree on and be united around "the message of the cross" (1 v 18), and not allow other issues to be divisive.

3. APPLY: When does respect for a Christian leader become unhealthy?
Opinions vary as to where proper respect for a Christian leader becomes unhealthy, and your group may differ slightly; that's fine! The important thing is to think about and discuss the issue. It is right to respect our Christian leaders and to submit to them under God. But it is unhealthy to:

• listen only to them and not other Christian leaders.
• listen to them simply because they have a more engaging style.
• believe what they say without checking it has come from Scripture.
• think that we are "better" Christians because we are friends with a particular leader.

4. What are the two reactions to the message of the cross (v 18)? The message of the cross was repulsive, "foolishness", to the ancient world. But to those in whose hearts God Himself was moving, it was the "power of God" (v 18).

⌄

• **What were people looking for instead of the message of the cross (v 22-23)?** Some wanted miracles: signs and proofs of God's power. So they rejected the cross because it told of a weak, crucified Christ. Others wanted wisdom: a message that was logical and fitted with worldly wisdom. So they rejected the cross because it challenged what "made sense" to them.

5. Will the Christian message ever sound impressive to the world? Why, or why not? The Christian message will never sound impressive in worldly terms—Christians will always be faithfully offensive as they exalt

the cross and say that the only hope is trusting in God alone through Christ alone, and that we do not save ourselves. Worldly wisdom is totally different to God's wisdom (v 20-21, 25), and so those who pursue worldly wisdom will think of the Christian message as "foolish", unimpressive, and unpersuasive.

These two types of wisdom are opposed to one another; so if a Christian leader begins to peddle a message which pleases the world, the true "foolish" gospel will be de-emphasized, compromised, or even replaced.

6. What can human wisdom never do? The question is, if the gospel is "foolishness", why not simply rely on the world's wisdom? Surely wisdom is better than foolishness? But human "wisdom" cannot know God (v 21)—no one, whether a wise man, a scholar or a philosopher (v 20), was looking for the one true God to become incarnate as a human and to bear our sins as a substitute by dying the death of an outcast traitor!

⌄

• **If human wisdom cannot work out how to know God, how can anyone get to know Him and His saving power?** Verse 18 tells us that it is the "message of the cross" that is how people discover the "power of God". It is through the Christian message—through preaching—that God makes Himself known to people.

7. APPLY: What is "the message of the cross"? Why does it appear foolish to people today? You may choose to spend a long time or a short time on what "the message of the cross" is, depending on whether your group's members are clear on this or would benefit from spending some time thinking about exactly what is meant by this phrase.

It's important to realize that when Paul says "the message of the cross", he means far more than just the fact that Jesus died on a cross; he is thinking of its significance. The message contains the truths that:

- God judges sinful humanity.
- God became man to bear that judgment Himself.
- The cross is therefore the only way anyone can be forgiven and have eternal life.

It may be worth looking at a verse of the Bible which sets out what the message of the cross is, eg: 1 Peter 3 v 18; 2 Corinthians 5 v 21.

In fact, the reasons people think the cross is foolish today are similar to why people did then (v 22-23). Some ask for proof of God, or miraculous "signs" ("I'd believe in God if He did something right now!" or "If there is a God, why doesn't He stop earthquakes?"). Some demand that God fits in with the way they look at the world, with "wisdom" ("Science has disproved the notion of a God" or "What your God says about relationships is clearly out of touch").

- **So what will often happen when we tell people about Jesus? How is this a challenge to us?** As Christians, we must realize that the world thinks the Christian message is foolish. We know this because Christ was rejected (2 v 8). If we try to peddle a message by what pleases the world, the true gospel will be compromised or replaced. These verses challenge us not to think we can talk about the cross and look wise to non-Christians at the same time; and not to keep quiet when we find that the world does not like the Christian message.

8. Had these Christians chosen God, or had He chosen them (v 26-28)? This is a very simple question, but the answer may be one which some Christians need to grapple with. You will know your group; you may be able to move on having understood the straightforward answer that God chose these people to be Christians—He called them (v 26-27).

Note: You may want to pause and explain what the Bible says about God choosing His people:

From a human perspective, we become Christians when we choose to put our faith in Jesus and His death; we "call on the name of our Lord", as Paul puts it in 1 v 2. But in fact, from heaven's perspective, God has chosen to give us faith and call us into His people. We are only able to choose God because He has chosen us. The only reason we choose to have faith in Jesus is because God has chosen to work in us through His Spirit to enable us to do that (as Paul points out in 2 v 12 and v 14).

If this prompts some questions, a useful place to turn to in Scripture is Matthew 11 v 27-30. Here, Jesus states clearly that the only people able to know God are those to whom He chooses to reveal God (v 27); and then He calls people to choose to come to Him and know God (v 28). But this is not the main thrust of Paul's point here (so don't get too hung up on discussing it!)—the reason Paul mentions God's choice is to point out that... see the next question!

9. How impressive are these people by "human standards"? Why has God made the church like this? These Corinthians were nothing to write home about! Just by looking in the mirror they should see that God chooses the foolish and weak—not the impressive. And so the church will never look impressive by "human standards".

God has done this deliberately:
- to show the limits of what the world considers wise and impressive (v 27).
- so that no one could mistakenly think that their abilities or impressiveness had saved them and so boast about themselves instead of God (v 29).

10. Christian leaders will not sound impressive. Christian churches will not look impressive. Who are Christians to see as "impressive" (v 30-31)? We Christians should be humble about ourselves and our church leaders, and "boast in the Lord" (v 31). It is God who is truly impressive, and when things go well it is because God is behind it. It is "because of him (God) that you are in Christ Jesus" (v 30), not because of a wonderfully impressive church speaker.

⊠

- **What does boasting in the Lord mean in practical terms?** To talk about how great God is, and remember how great God is, rather than speak of ourselves or others as great.

11. If the whole church does as Paul tells them to in verse 31, why would that stop them being divided and help them stay united? Boasting only in God maintains unity because the church has a united focus—praising God. When your boasting is only in God, it's hard to get proud, or defensive, or divisive. So if things go well for us or for our church, this must be grounds for humility, not pride, as we remember that God is behind it.
Note: At this stage your group may ask you how this works when there are disagreements about style, theology or church practice. It is worth pointing out that

disagreement does not necessarily have to lead to division. If we agree over primary gospel issues (eg: who Jesus is; how we are saved; the truth that Jesus will return), then we should not divide over secondary issues (eg: the structure of our church services; the exact nature of our church governance; theological issues such as the order of events in Revelation—often called millenialism). Of course, sometimes it is hard to work out whether something is a primary gospel issue or a secondary one; but often churches are far too quick to divide over secondary issues (and, sometimes, far too slow to take a stand on primary ones).

12. How was Paul different to the spectacular, impressive-sounding speakers in Corinth? Paul couldn't have been more different! They aimed to gain a reputation more by their method of speech than what they said. Paul, on the other hand, did not preach with great eloquence or worldly wisdom (2 v 1), and he was weak in person (v 3). Paul let his weakness show so that their faith would correctly be based on God, not on his impressiveness or wisdom (v 5).

13. What did Paul think was most important about his ministry (v 2)? Paul saw his message as what mattered; and his message was that the man Jesus was the Christ, God's chosen King, and that he was crucified (2 v 2).

14. An unimpressive man, with an unimpressive message, delivered in an unimpressive way—why did Paul's words have any effect at all? What made Paul's preaching effective was "the Spirit's power" (v 4). The message and the man may have seemed unimpressive, but the Spirit works powerfully when the cross is preached, to call people to put their faith in Christ. Without the Spirit, Paul's preaching would have been useless.

It seems clear that the "demonstration of the Spirit's power" was not miracles, since Paul has already said that in Corinth the Jews demanded miracles (v 22), but all that Paul offered was preaching "Christ crucified". It's most likely that the Spirit's power was seen in people being saved (v 18). And what power, to work through an unimpressive-looking man with an unimpressive-sounding message!

15. APPLY: Imagine you found yourself moving to another community and looking for a new church. What should you look for most of all? Simply that Christ and Him crucified is clearly preached. This is what a church should be united around, and should intend to be committed to in everything from its hymns to its prayers to its preaching. This is far more important than styles of music, size of church, type of church government (ie: how the church is run), time of service, type of coffee, etc!

EXPLORE MORE
Read 1 Corinthians 2 v 6-16. Where does true wisdom come from, and what is it like (v 6-8)?
How do we get this type of wisdom?
Paul says in 2 v 6-9 that there is a wisdom that he taught, but that it is of God, that it is eternal, that it is secret, and that it tells of great good coming from God to us.
This wisdom from God comes by the Holy Spirit (v 10), who enables us to understand it (v 12).

GETTING PERSONAL
Once your group have had a chance to think individually about the Getting Personal section, it's worth talking about

and acknowledging together how much time we spend listening to the world (and thinking about how we listen); and perhaps committing to spending more time listening to God. It might be worth mentioning possible practical ways to do this:

• listening to the Bible on an mp3 player or at home
• talking with other Christians about films, TV shows, books etc, to help each other work out which parts of what they say are truly wise (because they reflect the teaching of Scripture) and which are foolish
• listening to Christian music rather than only secular music
• meeting up with a Christian friend to read the Bible together weekly
• memorizing Bible verses
• going to church twice instead of once on a Sunday.

At the end of the study, come back to Q1 and ask the group: What should decide whether or not we listen to someone's opinions? Whether they base what they say on Jesus being God's crucified King, regardless of whether they sound or look impressive in the eyes of non-Christians around us or our society.

OPTIONAL EXTRA
Record a clip of a TV show or film which you think offers some opinions which are wise (ie: agree with what God says in the Bible) and some which are foolish, but widely accepted. Possible programs include TV chat shows, particularly where "experts" offer to help ordinary people with their life issues; or a news program in which a panel give their views on a moral issue.
Show the clip to your group, and then ask them to help each other think through what was wise, and what was foolish.

3
1 Corinthians 3
UNITE AS GOD'S COMMUNITY

THE BIG IDEA

God lives among His people, the church. He directs its growth, and He owns it—so His people should be united in loving and worshipping Him, and no one else.

SUMMARY

Paul's thought in this section is continuing from 1 v 10, where he appealed to the Corinthian Christians to be united. The kind of division that they were experiencing showed a spiritual immaturity. They were living with the perspectives of Corinth, and their jealousy and quarreling proved it!

Paul sets out his argument that God directs the various workmen He employs (v 5-9), and God has the right to do this because, as Paul says in v 10-15, God founded the church. He set the foundation on Christ alone (v 11). In v 16-20 Paul points to the fact that God owns His fellowship—the local community of believers is God's temple, His chosen earthly home.

In all this, we are being encouraged to consider the importance of Christ to the church, and the importance of the church to God.

GUIDANCE ON QUESTIONS

1. Describe in one sentence what you think "church" is. There are many views of what "church" is, and there may well be a variety in the group—at this stage there are no "right" answers. If time allows, you may like to come back to this question at the end of the study and encourage the group to use this passage to come up with a one-sentence description of the church.

2. How does Paul describe these Christians (v 1)? Spiritual infants—they are "worldly" people. They need to grow up!

3. What are the visible signs of this (v 3-4)? Their jealousy and quarreling about which leader was superior, which should be followed, whose baptism was superior (see 1 v 13-15), proved that these Christians were living just like those around them in Corinth, outside their fellowship. They had had good enough teaching from Paul and others to know better than to have divisions within the church. Paul is calling them to grow up!

☒

- **Why do we sometimes end up concentrating on or even celebrating differences between us and other Christians or churches?** Divisions can make us feel like "better" or "purer" Christians. Some of us have characters that mean we are quicker to spot differences than what unites us. Sometimes we can feel threatened by another Christian or church and rather than learning from them and being challenged by them, it can be easier to dismiss them.

4. In verses 5-9, how does Paul describe:
- **God?** The one "who makes things grow" (v 7)—people coming to Christ and growing in Christ is God's work.

- **himself, Apollos and any other Christian worker?** Ministers such as Paul and Apollos are "only servants" (v 5), God's "co-workers" (v 9).
Paul's point is that making too much of

ministers is to make too little of God. God in His kindness allows His people to plant seeds (evangelism) and water them (discipling), but it is God Himself who supplies the actual growth. In church growth, God is directing the various workmen that He employs.

• **How does this image encourage Christian leaders? How does it keep them humble?** It is a great privilege to be called a "co-worker" of God's (v 9), and to be used by Him for His purposes for His people. Yet it is God who is the master planter, the one "who makes things grow" (v 7)—compared to Him and His work, a minister is "nothing".

5. Who should Christians say they follow? Paul is pointing out that, both in their hearts and in what they say, Christians follow God! The kind of division this Christian community was facing was essentially an attack on God Himself, because He, not a particular leader, is to be the focus of a Christian's loyalty, obedience, hopes and praise. A believer should simply say: "I follow God".

6. APPLY: How would you encourage someone who said to you: *"I've given up telling people about Jesus. It just never seems to work. I'll never make anyone a Christian"*? They need to be reminded that they don't make people Christians: it is God who does this as He grows a seed. They need to keep planting seeds by telling people about Christ, and watering seeds by continuing to tell them about Christ; and they need to pray that God would give them the privilege of being used by Him, that He would grow the seed they've planted. Instead of giving up, they

need to pray and trust that God is at work, even when they can't see how.

7. As Paul looks forward to "the Day" that Jesus is revealed (1 v 7), what does he say will happen at that time:
• **v 12-13:** Each minister's work of church-building will be judged not on its superficial appearance, but on how consistent it is with this foundation.
Note: It is not completely clear from the passage what Paul means in v 12 by "gold, silver, costly stones, wood, hay or straw". What does it mean for a church leader to build with valuable materials or cheap goods? Probably, Paul wants church leaders to build on "this foundation" with the same materials the foundation is made out of, "which is Jesus Christ" (v 11). The cheaper stuff may well stand for building with human wisdom, not God's.

• **v 14-15:** Paul's encouragement to Christian fellowships (and particularly to their leaders) is that churches which are built on and with Christ will survive the "fire" of judgment, and those leaders will "receive [their] reward" (v 14); if on the other hand "it is burned up, [they] will suffer loss" (v 15). So when a church leader is judged by God, God will either say his ministry has been worthwhile (because it was all about Christ), and he will be rewarded in eternity; or that his ministry has not been Christ-centered, has therefore been useless, and has no place in God's eternal kingdom.
Note: It's important to notice, and to point out to your group if they are confused, that Paul is not talking here about whether particular leaders are saved or not. The "reward" is in eternal life, but it is not eternal life itself. So church leaders who are Christians but do not point to Christ

are themselves "saved—even though only as one escaping through the flames." Paul's focus is on what happens to their work, not on what happens to them.

☒

• **The image in v 5-9 was of a garden. How has Paul changed the image in v 10-15?** Paul's now picturing a building.

8. What is exciting about what Paul says in verse 16? Why is it a motivation to stay united? Verse 16 tells us that the local Christian community (that includes you!) is God's temple. In Old Testament Israel, the temple in Jerusalem was the place where God dwelled among His people in His world; now the place where God dwells in His world is His people, through His Spirit (see Ephesians 2 v 19-22). This should cause us excitement and a sense of privilege and responsibility, for our church (the people, not the building!) is where God lives and is where God can be seen.

If the fellowship is God's house, it needs to be united, since a divided house is not much of a house at all. Unity is necessary to make God's temple a home fit for such an awesome owner.

OPTIONAL EXTRA

You might like to draw a picture of Paul's thought in v 10-16, or to get your group to, in order to visualize it. Paul is describing the church as a house, with Christ as its foundation, laid by God through Paul. It is built (hopefully!) with materials which match the foundation ie: precious teaching about, and worship of, Jesus. But this house is made from people—Christians who have been taught the truth about Jesus Christ and His death (2 v 2). And it is God's house, built of people who trust in Christ crucified.

☒

• **How important is the church to God (v 17)?** Division such as seen in the Corinthian church can wound and even kill a local congregation—and God says that He Himself will destroy a person who destroys His church. He cares deeply!

9. How have verses 5-17 shown the foolishness of doing this [boasting about their relationship with a particular Christian leader]? Because:
• *God* directs His church's growth; not a particular leader (v 6).
• *God* founded the church on Christ; this was through a leader, but it was His work (v 10-11).
• *God* dwells in the church as His temple, and it belongs to Him; not a particular leader (v 16-17).
• *God* is therefore the one who the Christian follows and looks to; not a particular leader (v 21).

10. In verses 21-23, what does Paul say these Christians have? True Christians already have everything! They have all the riches of Christ—so Paul is able to say "all things are yours" (as he's already said in 1 v 5). There is no need for division caused by loyalty to different leaders, because God has given all these leaders to the church. By being loyal to God, they can benefit from all of them!

Note: Paul extends his thinking here from simply the different leaders in the Corinthian church to the whole of the world and eternity. "All things are yours," he says— because Christians belong to Christ, and Christ belongs to God, and all these things are under God's control (just as the church and its leaders are).

11. What three warnings does Paul give them in this section?

- **v 10, 13:** To "build with care" (v 10). This is particularly aimed at anyone who has any kind of ministry among their fellowship (be it up-front teaching or welcoming at the door or encouraging others). The right materials to build with are consistent with the foundation God has laid, "which is Jesus Christ" (v 11).

- **v 17:** Not to destroy the community by dividing it (v 17). Church disunity and splits are tragically common; the Christian is not to provoke or encourage them. (This is not to say that a split is always wrong. False teaching must be resisted, even if it means division. But this was clearly not the reason Christians in Corinth were divided among themselves.)

- **v 18:** Not to deceive themselves by thinking that because they were wise in the world's eyes, they were wise in God's (v 18). Paul encourages believers to humble themselves before God's word (even though that means looking foolish to the world). Then they will be able to gain godly wisdom. In many ways this last section (v 18-23) looks back to the passage covered in the previous study, especially 1 v 18-25 and 2 v 6-16.

⊻

- **What does it mean to become a "fool"?** Here Paul is looking back to what he wrote in the previous section, especially 1 v 18-25 and 2 v 6-16. To become a "fool" is to listen to and accept God's teaching, rather than thinking, as the world does, that we know better.

12. What three things is Paul telling us about God's relationship to the church?

Paul has established three great truths about the community of God from His point of view (which should be our point of view too!):

- **v 6-9:** God directs it; He is the grower, working through His servants and behind the scenes (v 6-9).

- **v 10:** God founded it; in His kindness He worked through Paul to lay the foundation of Jesus Christ (v 10-11). Notice Paul acknowledges that he should not get the credit for setting up the Corinthian church; it was "by the grace *God* has given me".

- **v 16:** God owns it; the local church is His temple, as He lives in His people by His Spirit (v 16).

Return to Q1 at the beginning of the study. Using this passage, ask your group (perhaps in pairs) to sum up in a sentence what church is.

13. APPLY: Using this passage, how would you respond to a friend who said:

- **"I really only like to listen to (insert name of preacher); he's just so much more inspiring and interesting than any other speaker I've heard"?** (The Apply section gives your group the chance to respond to two "people". Encourage the group to point out which verses they would use to respond to each one.)

This "voice" is being divisive by being loyal to a particular church leader rather than to God. Verses 5-9 will remind them that their leader is only a servant of God, and that it's God who works through him to grow Christians. God can work through other leaders too, even if they're not such gifted orators. By making this particular leader so much in their mind, they are making God less.

- **"We spend too much time thinking about what church should be like: we need just to get out there and tell people about Christ"?** This person should be encouraged in their desire to get out there and preach Christ Jesus and Him crucified! But they also need to take the community of God's people

seriously, because God does. Church is not an afterthought to God; He cares deeply about His temple, and what happens in it and how His people act towards others in it. Just as we care about what our homes look like and how people act in them, so God cares about His church (ie: His people) and what goes on in it!

1 Corinthians 4

4 RECOGNIZE REAL MINISTERS

THE BIG IDEA

Real Christian ministers are cross-centered in their message, in how they live, and in how they encourage and challenge their followers to live.

SUMMARY

Paul is concerned about imposters in Corinth who were leading the young Christians astray by teaching them a substitute message and so obscuring the gospel of "Jesus Christ and him crucified" (2 v 2). It is not clear what this false message was, but it may well have been something to do with "spiritual kingship", the notion that God's promised, future glorified recreation could be experienced straight away in this life. This would be why Paul sarcastically describes them as "rich" and "reigning" (4 v 8).

The results of their presence, their words, even their actions, would be terrible for themselves, and for all those around them. For a short amount of worldly glory, they and those who followed their words would be repaid by eternal grief.

So, to enable these Corinthian Christians to spot the real, faithful minister from the fake

imposter, Paul gives them three key qualities of a real minister:

- **A cross-centered message:** (v 1-7) A minister is all about communicating "the mysteries God has revealed" (v 1), the gospel of the crucified Christ. And they are required to be faithful to the God who's given them this message. Paul talks about whose judgment he cares about in v 3-5, and ultimately God's is the only one that matters, since God is his boss, not the church or the world.

- **A cross-centered life:** In v 8-13, Paul uses lots of irony. The Corinthians prioritized prosperity, whether real or imagined; presumably the fake ministers told them to, and enjoyed prosperity themselves. But Paul's life was a little more humble. Paul carried his cross: he suffered cursing and persecution and poverty, just as Christ had. He lived a life which showed there were things worth more than this world's wealth.

- **Encouraging cross-centered followers** is the third key quality of a real minister. Paul writes: "I urge you to imitate me" (v 16). A Christian pastor is called to lead others to live out a Christlike life, and Paul wants his spiritual children (v 14-15) to copy him. And being this kind of church leader means treating Christians with gentleness and severity, as appropriate. So Paul will come "with a rod of discipline" (v 21) if necessary, because he desperately wants to see these young Christians listening to and influenced by real, faithful ministers, instead of fake, disastrous ones.

OPTIONAL EXTRA

Buy some real Coca-Cola, and buy some "alternatives" (Diet, Zero, other brands). Put them all in unmarked cups, and let your group taste each one of them. The challenge is to work out which is the real Coca-Cola, and which are the "fakes". Talk about what you are looking for in terms of taste as you seek to discern the "real" Coca-Cola. (You might like to include one drink which is completely obviously "fake", like orange juice.)

GUIDANCE ON QUESTIONS

1. What makes a good church minister? What should their priorities be? This is to encourage the group to think about what actually makes a good minister. It would be helpful to keep the conversation general rather than specific to a particular pastor; and positive rather than negative! Your group may come up with many qualities and characteristics, in which case you might like to ask them what are the top three priorities of a good minister?

2. What do those who have been entrusted with church leadership need to do (v 2)? A minister must be faithful. Ministers are like bankers; given a great deposit by someone to take care of. So pastors must be faithful in their work because of the great value of what has been entrusted to them.

If someone asks what it means to be "faithful", encourage them to wait for Q5, which describes part of what faithful ministry involves.

3-4. Whose judgments does Paul not care about (v 3)? Whose judgment does Paul care about, and when will this judgment happen (v 5)? Paul's point here is that ministers are judged by whether they are faithful to their master, God. A church leader is not working for their congregation, and so their judgment is not ultimately what matters. Certainly what the world thinks does not matter. And even what the minister himself thinks doesn't matter—their conscience may be clear, but God may not agree! Self-esteem cannot be the final arbiter of judgment. It's right to make provisional judgments (as 1 Corinthians 5 will show), but no human can be our ultimate judge, because, as Paul says, all leaders (and all people) will be judged by the Lord. This judgment will happen when "the Lord comes" (v 5).

⊻

• **Does this mean that if I have a ministry and someone criticizes it, I can or should ignore them?** No! If someone has a negative comment about your ministry, with which you instinctively disagree, that doesn't mean you can ignore what they say—your conscience may be clear, but you could still be wrong (v 4). The important question is whether their judgment is reflective of God's judgment. If they are criticizing you for preaching Jesus as Christ or Jesus' death on the cross, then their judgment should be ignored. If the criticism centers on how you are conducting your ministry, then they may have a point and you need to be humble enough to consider their comments.

5. Paul has said ministers must be "faithful"; and verse 6 tells us some of what it means to be faithful. What should Paul, Apollos and any other church leader *not* do? Paul and Apollos must not "go beyond what is written"; and nor must any church leader today. Ministers should be careful to be faithful in delivering God's message. All true Christian teachers have been commissioned by the same Master for the same purpose—to teach His truth.

6. Paul summed up the content of God's message in 2 v 2. What is it? That Jesus is the Christ, God's chosen King, and that the Christ was crucified, dying to bear the punishment sinners deserve so that they can have forgiveness and eternal life.

7. APPLY: Why might it be tempting for a church minister to "go beyond what is written" (4 v 6)? There are various reasons why a minister might go beyond what is written, and your group may come up with some not listed here:
• To sound impressive and knowledgeable
• Out of a desire to attract people to church by promising them more than God has promised
• Because their superiors in their church hierarchy are doing so
• Because their congregation demand knowledge on a certain point not covered in Scripture
• Out of a desire to give comfort to someone who is facing a difficult situation

⌄

• **Why might church leaders not "go up to" what is written? Why might they leave some Bible truths out of their teaching?** Many, many reasons! Common ones may include:
• A desire not to offend
• Wanting the gospel to sound attractive to outsiders, so they change it slightly
• Pressure to conform to society's current "wisdom"
• Because church members don't like a difficult teaching
• Because they are not willing to rebuke and challenge

8. APPLY: How can we help our pastors make sure they don't do this? Again, see how your group feel they can help their minister in your particular church. Some ideas for how to help ministers teach all that is written but not go beyond it include:
• Keep your Bible open during sermons and check you can find what's being preached in the passage.
• Be reading your Bible regularly, so you know it well enough to compare what's being said with what God says.
• Ask respectfully and gently after a service if you are concerned something unbiblical was said.
• Thank your minister when he preaches truths clearly that challenge or rebuke you.

9. Pick out how Paul describes: (Paul sets up a contrast in v 8-10. On the one side is what the Corinthians think of themselves, or at least want to achieve through living the Christian life. On the other side is what Paul's life is like as a real, faithful minister.)

The Corinthians' view of themselves	Paul's view of himself
Rich (v 8)	End of the procession (v 9—see note below)
Reigning (v 8)	A spectacle (v 9)
Wise (v 10)	Fool (v 10)
Strong (v 10)	Weak (v 10)
Honored (v 10)	Dishonored (v 10)

Note: In New Testament times, the defeated army in battle would be marched into the victorious city by the triumphant army. At the head of the procession would come the king. The prisoners came last in line, and very last of all came the lowest in rank and most despised. Often they would be "condemned to die".

⊗

• **In what ways today can churches try to teach and live as Christians "without us" (v 8) ie: without Paul?** Paul's teachings are often unfashionable both in society and within churches today! In areas of sexual morality, the role of men and women, what Jesus did on the cross, God's just judgment, and others, God speaks through Paul in a way which disagrees with many of the assumptions of 21st-century life.

Some churches ignore Paul's teachings, never preaching or teaching the more "difficult" passages; some focus solely on the four Gospels; some openly contradict Paul's teachings, arguing that he is not consistent with what Jesus said in the Gospels.

All this, of course, ignores the fact that Paul was "called to be an apostle of Christ Jesus by the will of God" (1 v 1), and deliberately based all his teaching on

"Jesus Christ and him crucified" (2 v 2). To try to teach Christianity while ignoring God's messenger, Paul, is to not teach Christianity at all; to disagree with Paul's writings is to disagree with God.

10. It appears the fake teachers had been promising the Corinthians wealth and power. How does Paul's life show that these are false promises? Paul believed that he had no right to expect well-wishes from God-haters, no ultimate right to freedom or to a good name among those who rejected Christ. The world cursed him, persecuted him, and slandered him. And this showed up the falseness of the fake preachers' promises. If Christianity led to riches and power, then Paul was not a Christian!

Many churches today have been attracted to what is often called the "prosperity gospel"—that following Christ brings material wealth. These verses clearly show that this "gospel" is not the biblical one—it is false teaching. See also Mark 10 v 17-31; 2 Corinthians 11 v 21b-33; Revelation 3 v 14-21.

11. Paul describes his experience of real Christian ministry. Read Luke 9 v 58 and 1 Peter 2 v 21-24. How is minister Paul's experience similar to that of his Master—Jesus Christ? Jesus had no home of His own, and sometimes no welcome in anyone else's home. Jesus, when He went to the cross, was insulted but did not retaliate, and He suffered but didn't threaten His enemies. The cross was, ultimately, the reason He came to earth and the climax of His ministry.

Paul's experience in v 11-13 is similar: he is hungry, in rags, mistreated, homeless, cursed (but he blesses), persecuted (but he endures it) and slandered (but he's kind in return). So as a Christian minister, he has given up much, just as his Master did.

⊻

• **How does 1 Peter 2 v 23b link to 1 Corinthians 4 v 3-5?** Jesus bore the wrong judgment of the Jewish and Roman leaders. He did this because the judgment He cared about was the verdict of His Father, who "judges justly". And in the same way we've seen that Paul did not care what judgments the world made about him, because the only judgment he was concerned with was God's. In this, again, Paul lives a Christ-like life.

And so living a cross-centered, Christ-like life is the second key quality of a real minister.
Note: This does not mean that all ministers must be homeless and dress only in rags, though they should be prepared to if necessary. The real minister must no longer be concerned with the world's wisdom, a world that made the decision to crucify Christ (2 v 8). They will no longer live for what a world that opposes God calls "strength". They will not be aiming for applause and honor from those who have rejected Jesus. True ministers are happy to be despised if, by their being despised, somehow the gospel is displayed.

12. How does Paul describe his relationship with the Corinthians? Why does he think of himself in this way? Paul says he is the Corinthians' "father". He thinks of himself like this because, as he reminds them, he is uniquely their father in the gospel. Paul was the church planter of the church in Corinth, the founding father (under God) of that local congregation. There should be a special place in people's

hearts for those whom God used to bring them to Christ.
They may have many "guardians" (other good teachers), but they'll only ever have one "father".

13. Paul lives a cross-centered life. What kind of life does he want the Christians in his care to have (v 16)? The Christians in Corinth are to imitate Paul. And so this means them living a cross-centered life too. The Christian minister is called not only to teach and live out a Christlike life, but also to lead others to do the same. Church leaders are models.
Note: You might want to point your group to 1 Corinthians 11 v 1, in which Paul makes clear he wants the church to imitate him only because he imitates Christ. Jesus is the ultimate One who His people are to imitate.

14. APPLY: Based on this passage, how would you respond to these two situations: (These two "voices" are to help your group think about how the passage could guide their responses to others in their church family, and to themselves if necessary. Encourage the group members to state the verses in the passage they're drawing their response from, so that their answers come from what they've seen in the session rather than simply from what they knew—or thought they knew!— already.)

• **After the church service, a member of your small group is annoyed with the minister.** *"I can't believe he said that sex outside marriage is wrong,"* she says. *"I mean, life's more complicated than that, isn't it? And I've got a friend visiting who doesn't come to church much; what's he going to think? Why can't the pastor tone it down a bit?"* This person needs to be reminded that a faithful church leader will preach Christ crucified and encourage followers to lead a sacrificial, cross-centered life. God's judgment matters much more than the judgment of her friend, or of the world. The minister would not be being faithful to what is written in God's word if he "toned it down a bit".

• **A friend from church has bought a brand new sports car. *"I wasn't sure about getting it, but then I realized God would want me to buy it," he tells you. "God has given us all good things as part of His promise to us in the gospel, hasn't He? It's right that His people enjoy the wealth He has given us."*** The gospel does promise us, in the final resurrection, freedom from all suffering and the riches of God's presence. Jesus' body is the first-fruits of this. But we must not fall into the trap this church had, of thinking that the Christian life will bring riches now; the real Christian life is a cross-centered life, not a credit-card-centered one. The hypothetical speaker here is correct that all the good things we have come from God, and are to be "received with thanksgiving" (1 Timothy 4 v 3); but that does not mean the Christian should chase worldly possessions and pleasures. Quite the reverse. It's in the gospel itself, not in wealth, that God provides us with everything we need to know joy (1 Timothy 6 v 17). Prosperity is not always wrong, but it is always dangerous. It can be disorienting to the Christian. Christians must live lives that show there are things that are worth even more than this world's prosperity.

You might like to encourage your group to think of themselves as ministers to one another, in the sense that as they speak to one another about these issues (and others), they have an opportunity to point to the cross-centered message, live out the cross-centered life themselves and encourage others to do the same: in other words, be real ministers to one another.

EXPLORE MORE
When Paul revisits Corinth, what are the two options for how he treats these Christians (v 21)? He will come with gentleness or with a "whip" (v 21), by which he means a severe reproof. The way in which the believers prepare for his coming will determine the nature of Paul's visit. He's like a loving father who longs to be gentle, but who for the sake of his children's integrity is prepared to be tough. This is a good reminder that both gentleness and severity are part of Christian love and leadership.

PRAY

Before the study, you could ask your minister(s) for some other prayer points for them and their families, which you could then move on to when you have finished praying through what the passage says.

5

1 Corinthians 5–6

DON'T GO SOFT ON SIN

THE BIG IDEA

Churches and individual Christians must not be complacent about sin among their members, but expose and discipline those who are sinning, both to help those who Christ has died for to live purely, and to witness effectively to those outside the church.

SUMMARY

In this section Paul is dealing with the tricky issue of what to do about public and unrepentant sin within the congregation. The Corinthian church is proud of its tolerance of such sin (v 2): Paul insists instead they must judge it as sinful, and if necessary excommunicate the individual(s) involved. He warns them not to be complacent about sin within the church, but to expose and discipline those who are sinning.

Paul gives the church several reasons why it's crucial to be clear about sin, and deal with it: for the good of the sinner, so that he is forced to realize that his actions aren't in line with the lifestyle of someone Christ has died for; for the church, so that this sin would not spread throughout its membership; and for outsiders, so that they would be able to see Christlikeness as they look at the church.

Sin matters—it leaves us outside God's kingdom (6 v 9-10). But the wonderful truth of the gospel is that sinners have been cleansed and forgiven through Christ (v 11).

This is a long study. You might wish to split it into two sessions, after Q7.

GUIDANCE ON QUESTIONS

1. *"It's not right to judge what anyone

else does." **Do you agree or disagree? Would there be any situations in which you'd change your answer?** In today's culture we have backed ourselves into a corner when it comes to judging. We discourage judgmental statements, but our lives require evaluations all the time. Allow your group to talk this over for a fair amount of time (while leaving time for the study itself!) Allow disagreement, and don't push for "right" answers. Make sure everyone who wants to has contributed on the first part of the question before moving on to think about situations where people would change their answer.

The final Apply question (Q12) picks up on this same statement, in light of the passage.

2. What has Paul heard has happened within this church? Sexual immorality appears to be common; and there's even incest of a kind that was forbidden in Roman law. In fact, one could be expelled from the city of Corinth for engaging in it.

- **How have the other church members react (v 2)?** The church welcomed the sinning believer while being fully aware of what was going on. They were proud about being so tolerant, and may even have been boasting about their acceptance of the sin itself.

3. What should they be doing (v 2)? Instead of pride, there should be great mourning that a Christian brother has fallen into such serious sin. And Paul exhorts them to excommunicate this man. Note that this is a whole-church matter; excommunication is not the job of a clique. Excommunication must never be heartless; it should always be accompanied by grief.

⌄

• **What does it actually look like to "[go] into mourning" about a fellow Christian's sin, do you think?**

4. What does Paul hope this (handing the man "over to Satan") will result in (end of verse 5)? That he will, in the end, be saved from God's judgment when Christ returns. Dealing with sin that hasn't been isolated and exposed is difficult, much like seeing something which is invisible or hearing something which is inaudible. Excommunicating someone was both a statement that the church regarded such unrepented sin as serious, and that such behavior was incompatible with being part of God's people (see verses 9-10); and it aimed at shocking this man into realizing what he was doing, and returning to his Lord and to His people.
Note: Excommunication would not necessarily have forbidden the man to attend public services; he was simply not to be regarded as a church member, and he was therefore not to participate in the privileges of membership, especially in the Lord's Supper.

5. Read Matthew 18 v 15-17. How are Paul's commands to this church reflecting Jesus' teaching during His time on earth? Sin is to be dealt with, if possible, by those it affects (v 15). It's then to be dealt with by a small group (v 16). But because all individual sin affects the church as a whole, it is ultimately a whole-church matter, and if a church member won't repent even when called to by the whole church, Jesus tells His people to treat that

person as though they were not a follower of His (v 17).
Paul's command is not directed to the elders but to the congregation as a whole. The entire church has a responsibility not to tolerate unrepentant sin. In both Jesus' and Paul's teaching, the final word is left to the assembly as a whole.

6. If it's not dealt with, what will happen (v 6)? It will work its way through the whole church, just as a tiny amount of yeast works through a whole batch of dough. Paul is warning against being complacent about the effect even a "small amount" of sin can have on a congregation. If not dealt with, then the attitude of other church members to sin generally will be compromised, as it will seem that sin doesn't matter much; and it may be that that specific sin will be copied by other Christians too.
The man's sin was a single serious infection, but the church's lack of discipline was a complete failure of the immune system. Sin that no one deals with becomes sin that everyone will have to deal with.

EXPLORE MORE
How does Paul refer to Christ in verse 7?
Our Passover lamb.
What did the blood of the Passover lamb achieve for God's people in Egypt?
By sacrificing a lamb and putting its blood on their doors, they escaped God's judgment when it fell. They were freed to leave Egypt (v 17), and to enter and enjoy the land the LORD had promised to give them (v 25).
What was the significance of yeast in the feast at which God's people showed their thanks for Him rescuing them from Egypt (v 17-20)? The people were to live without yeast. Not only was it not to be in

the bread they ate (v 18), but it was not even to be in their houses (v 19). This was a way of the people showing that they were God's rescued people.

How should Christians, who Christ has died for, show they are part of His people today (1 Corinthians 5 v 8)? Christians are called to contribute the unleavened bread to the Passover Feast, knowing that God's only Son has become our Passover lamb. The way to do this, Paul says, is by getting the yeast of sin out of our church. The Lamb has been slain—our participation at the feast is by making our communities ones of "sincerity and truth" rather than "malice and wickedness".

7. APPLY: Many Christians instinctively don't want to think about discipline or confront public sin. Why do you think this is? There are many reasons, both on an individual and a church level. Let the group discuss it in terms of their own context, but some possibilities are: because we (rightly) prize unity, and sometimes forget that unity is to be in the truth; because we underestimate the seriousness of sin; because we don't want to seem judgmental or harsh; because we are worried about what others will think of us; because the person needing discipline might be our friend, and we end up valuing their friendship more than we do our church's purity and that person's faith.

• **If there were no biblical church discipline in your church, what might the result be?** Similar to in Corinth! Without any kind of church discipline, sin comes to be seen as not particularly serious; and particular sins can quickly spread through the congregation.

Note: Different churches and denominations practise discipline and confront sin in

different ways. Your group's church will have its own way of doing things. You may like to talk to your church pastor before this study to find out how your church organises discipline; and to direct group members to him if they have specific questions. For your group, what's important is to see the principles of church discipline in Scripture, and to see (both from 1 Corinthians 5 and Matthew 18) that they have a responsibility as a church member.

If you want to break this session into two, this would be a good place.

8. Paul reminds his readers "not to associate with sexually immoral people" (v 9). What _doesn't_ he mean by this (v 10)? Paul is quick to clarify that he is not referring to those outside the church, to non-Christians (otherwise many Christians would struggle to be able to spend time with anyone around them who wasn't a Christian!)

• **What _does_ he mean (v 11)?** Paul is writing about church members. If a fellow church member is living in a way which is publicly sinful, Christians should "not even eat" with them. This obviously means the Lord's Supper (see 11 v 17-34)—but also eating at home. The unrepentant sinner needs to see that they have been excommunicated from fellowship. And Christians are to eat and drink "for the glory of God" (10 v 31), and cannot do this if they have invited an unrepentant church member to eat with them, and so are quietly allowing rebellion against God to go unchallenged by pretending nothing is wrong.

This is not to say that we must never speak to or spend time with that member—we may want to challenge them, and call them to repentance, and encourage them to see that they can be forgiven by turning back to Christ—but we must not by our actions look as though we are tacitly accepting how they are living.

9. Whose business *isn't* it for the church to judge (v 12)? Who will do this? Those outside of the church: they will face God's judgment when Christ returns.

• **Whose business *is* it for the church to judge?** God has called on us to act on His behalf inside the church, expelling the "wicked" from our midst. Paul is writing to this church about defaulting on their responsibility to take care of what goes on inside.

• **But the church is often tempted to judge the world while refusing to judge itself. Why do you think this is?** One writer says: "The ease with which the present-day church often passes judgment on the ethical or structural misconduct of the outside community is at times matched only by its reluctance to take action to remedy the ethical conduct of its own members" (Bruce Winter).
The reasons for this may well be similar to the answers to Q7. In particular, though, it is much easier to judge those we don't know than those we do; and if we are willing to call sin sin within the church community, then we are accepting that others have the right to do that for us and about our behavior, too.
To refuse to judge sin in the church is to obscure the gospel, harm ourselves, especially the weakest and most vulnerable among us—those trapped in their sin—and to dishonor God Himself. It has been said that when discipline leaves a church, Christ goes with it.

EXPLORE MORE
What has been going on in the Corinthian church (v 1, 6)? Christians had been taking their internal disputes to be settled in the city courts, before outsiders.
What attitude does Paul recommend instead (v 7)? Acting in humility towards each other, and for the good of others. It is better to be wronged than to obscure our witness to outsiders. The Corinthian Christians were not content to be wronged, so they chose to wrong someone else.
What will inspire Christians to give up what they deserve, instead of insisting on it? Christ went the way of complete self-giving. If we claim to follow Christ, we need to be willing to go the way He went; and His example will inspire us to do so.

10. Why does sin matter so much (v 9-10)? The result of continuing in sin is that that individual won't be saved. The stakes are high.

• **If a church does not discipline people who live like that, they might be "deceived" (v 9) into thinking it's fine. Why does this matter?** Because then they will think they are Christians, and so saved, when in fact their lifestyle suggests that they're not really followers of Christ, and so will not "inherit the kingdom". The German pastor, Dietrich Boenhoffer, once commented: "Nothing can be more cruel than the tenderness that consigns another to his sin. Nothing can be more compassionate than the severe rebuke that calls a brother back from the path of sin." We must welcome all, but not love their sin.

• **What is the great news Paul reminds them about?** Verse 11—that people who live like that, and are heading for being shut out of God's kingdom, can be "washed... sanctified... justified in the name of (ie: through recognising and knowing) the Lord Jesus Christ" and the work of His Spirit.

- **Why does Paul repeat the word "were" in verse 11, do you think?** To underline that being made right with God and found not guilty before Him is not a process, but an event in the Christian's past. Whatever sin lies behind the Christian, and whatever sin the Christian battles with each day, they have already been given a place in God's eternal kingdom.

11. Paul gives four reasons why sexual immorality really *does* matter. Each one is a really exciting truth about God! Pick them out: See table below.

Q12. APPLY: *"It's not right to judge people."* What would Paul say to your church about this attitude? Refer back to Q1, and encourage people to look back over the passage to shape their answer (which may or may not have changed). Key points:

- It's vital to call sin sin, which involves judging people's actions (5 v 2, 4-6)
- We're to be more concerned with judging each other within the church than we are judging the actions and attitudes of those outside the church (5 v 12-13)
- We should prefer to miss out ourselves than to ask outsiders to judge between us and a fellow Christian (6 v 7-8).

- **What part must each individual church member play in keeping their church pure?** You might want to remind the group of Jesus' words in Matthew 18. We are each to help each other not to sin; and then we need to support our church leaders if they decide to discipline someone for clear and unrepented sin.

	Truth about God	Why it shows sexual immorality matters
v 14	He raises people (physically)	If my eternal state will be in my body, what I do with my body is important!
v 15-16	We are joined to Christ	I represent Christ in this world; and what I do with my body, I'm doing with something that is part of Christ
v 18-19a	God's Spirit lives in us: we are where God lives on earth	It's using God's house to sin!
v 19b-20	God paid a price to buy us (ie: we are redeemed by Jesus' death, see Colossians 1 v 13-14)	Our bodies don't belong to us, but to God.

6
1 Corinthians 7
LET YOUR CALLING COUNT

THE BIG IDEA
Instead of seeking to change our circumstances to bring us satisfaction, we're to be satisfied by our identity as people called to know God. And whether we are currently single, married or widowed, we're to use our circumstances to serve God.

SUMMARY
Underlying Paul's instructions to married people, and to single people (whether single because they are unmarried or widowed), is his desire for Christians to make serving God their priority. In a world which strives to change its circumstances in order to find satisfaction, Christians are to accept their circumstances and to remember that first and foremost they are not married, single or widowed, Jew or Gentile, slave or free—they are people called by God (v 17-24). This is where we find our identity and satisfaction.

Paul addresses a variety of different circumstances and sets out how an individual in that situation can serve God. Married Christians are to serve one another, including in bed (v 3-5). Those married to non-Christians are to remain committed to their marriage (v 12-14), unless their spouse leaves them (or their spouse staying would require compromising their faith and obedience to God—v 15-16).

Singleness is, Paul says, a gift (v 7); it means avoiding the troubles of marriage (v 28) and provides greater opportunity to serve the Lord (v 32-35). Widows are likewise to use their singleness to serve God, but are free to remarry a Christian (v 39—as, it seems, are Christians whose non-believing spouse has left them, v 15).

These are tricky and emotive issues, and it's likely your group will have a variety of different experiences, joys and regrets when it comes to relationships. This section of the Bible should be encouraging to all, that the relationship which matters most is that with God, which He has called them to, and which they will enjoy eternally, no matter what the frustrations and pain imperfect human relationships (or lack of them) cause them now.

GUIDANCE ON QUESTIONS
1. If you surveyed 100 people in your area, asking them what they needed to make them happy, what would the most popular answers be? Most people tend to think that worldly circumstances are all-important, and that the problems we have will be solved, and increased happiness secured, by simply changing our circumstances. You will probably find that your group's answers are all circumstance-based—more money, bigger house, better car, different relationship status, more time, successful children—because we (in church as well as outside it) think of our marital status, our employment and our possessions as the all-important aspects of our lives, the things that determine our goodness, happiness and satisfaction.

2. What is the idea Paul repeats most often in v 17-24? Calling: that God called them to salvation (see 1 v 26-30).

- **What is [the point Paul is making about our identity]?** Our calling to God is primary, whatever our situation in life. Believers are to understand their call to God as the primary issue, and our relationship with God through Christ Jesus as what is most precious to us, which most defines us, and which should most shape our attitudes and emotions.

3. In v 22, what does Paul call slaves? What does he call those who are free? Slaves are God's freed people; equally, free people are "Christ's slaves".

• **What point do you think he making?** There is a liberty and a slavery that all Christians share. No matter what our earthly calling is, we are all God's freed people and His servants through Christ. We are to understand our calling to God as the most important thing, regardless of our situation in life (v 24).

Note: In first-century Corinth, slavery was not racial slavery, nor were all slaves completely "owned" by their masters as their property. Many if not most of the slaves had rights; they were essentially in an economic contract with their masters. It wasn't uncommon for people to sell themselves into slavery for the advantages that could be gained, and then to buy themselves out some years later. When we read Paul's words about slavery, we mustn't think he has the transatlantic slave trade in mind. And Paul is not advocating slavery, as is clear from his words in verse 21 that encourage a slave to obtain freedom if the opportunity arises. Verses 21 and 23, and his statement elsewhere forbidding slave trading (1 Timothy 1 v 10) effectively prohibit Christians from promoting slavery. Our circumstances are not unimportant; but they are not to be viewed as ultimate.

4. Why is being "called" by God more important than our circumstances (v 29, 31)? This life is not most of what

there is, and this world is not all that there is. It's much more important to be in relationship with God, called by Him, than to enjoy the very best the world can offer.

5. APPLY: Think back to Q1. What type of circumstances are those around us working hard to gain, or to keep? The area and culture you live in will shape answers to this. You might like to follow up this question by asking your group how they think the priorities and views of those around them affect their own attitudes.

• **Why will the answers to Q4 enable us to have a different perspective?** We live with the light of the future streaming back into the present. We know that Christ is returning and so this world is passing away, and this rearranges our priorities. We won't think that the answer to having a fulfilling, satisfying life lies in having different worldly circumstances. We won't restlessly seek a new job, a new social status, a spouse (or different spouse).

6. APPLY: The bulk of this chapter (which we'll look at next) is about marriage, sex and singleness. As we approach these difficult, emotional issues, why are the truths we've seen vital to keep in mind? Because we tend to think that worldly circumstances are all-important, and so conclude our problems will simply be solved by changing them. That means we can end up feeling that getting married, or divorced, or having more sex, is what we need. We need to remember that what we most need, and all we need, is what we already have—to be called by God, and be "washed… sanctified… justified in the name of the Lord Jesus Christ and by the Spirit of our God" (6 v 11).

7. What answer does Paul give (v 1-5) [to the idea that sex is unspiritual, and not right for Christians]? Paul affirms marriage (v 2), and exhorts the married to have sexual relations (v 3), perhaps because the believers in Corinth were (wrongly) denying it to their spouses.

• **What reasons does Paul give for getting married (v 2, 9)?** Because singleness is so dangerous sexually, and therefore spiritually. Sex drive can be a very powerful thing, and much better to be enjoying it in the way God intends, within marriage, than to be struggling to keep it under control outside marriage.

8. Paul turns to the issue of the ending of marriages. Use v 10-16 to complete the table.

	Situation	Command
v 10-11	Considering ending marriage	Don't! And if you do, don't marry again.
v 12-14	A Christian who has a non-Christian spouse	Don't leave them simply because they are not a Christian.
v 15-16	A Christian whose non-Christian spouse leaves them	Let them go. You're free to consider the marriage dissolved.
v 39-40	Widow (or widower)	Free to marry any Christian of the opposite sex; though fine to stay single.

EXPLORE MORE

What does Jesus teach about divorce in Matthew 19 v 4-6, and why? Divorce is an undoing of something God has done.

Marriage was part of His perfect creation (v 4-5); it's something that God is involved with, joining two people into one unit (v 6). Our starting point when thinking about divorce is that it is not right (though Jesus does give circumstances in which it is permitted, see below).

So, why does the law God gave to Moses accept the existence of divorce (v 8)? Because people's "hearts were hard". In giving the law to Israel, God was legislating for sinful people, and so the Old Testament law regulates divorce. This does not mean that God thinks divorce is fine.

Under what circumstances does Jesus say divorce is allowed (v 9)? Marital unfaithfulness. Some take this to include domestic violence. Notice also that in 1 Corinthians 7 v 12-13, Paul adds another circumstance in which divorce is an option for a Christian: where an unbelieving spouse walks out of the marriage.

Note: This is, of course, a very difficult issue for many. You will know your group, and know how carefully you need to handle this. It may be wise to talk to particular individuals before this study, so that they know the topic is coming up, and the shape of what will be said. You may also want to pick up individually with some members of your group afterwards.

How does the disciples' reaction in v 10 mirror Paul's words in 1 Cor 7 v 28?! Marriage is not easy! The disciples realize that there is no "backing out" from a marriage commitment: it really is a promise to stick with someone for better and for worse. Marriage brings many joys; but Christians should be realistic and accept that it may well also bring many troubles, as Paul points out in 1 Corinthians 7 v 28.

9. APPLY: Paul has laid out a Christian view of sex, marriage and divorce.

How is this different to the view of the society in which you live? Probably very different! Sex is for within marriage, not for outside (even if someone is "burning with passion", v 9). Marriage is lifelong and divorce is only permitted in a few very specific situations, not an option for anyone who finds they are unhappy with their spouse.

- **How is Paul's teaching guarding against us making:**
too much of marriage? Marriage is hard. And knowing God, having been called by Him, is far more valuable and vital than being married.

too little of marriage? Marriage is a gift; it is the place where loving sex can be enjoyed; and it is not to be thought about as a temporary state.

10. What does Paul say are the advantages of being single? An unmarried person is free to devote themselves to the Lord, while married people have to concern themselves with pleasing their spouses. A single person needs to consider no one else other than how to serve God; someone who is married needs to consider their spouse eg: in how they spend their time, or use their money, or plan for their future.

- **What do these verses add to Paul's view of singleness? v 26, 29-31:** "The present crisis" is the situation in which Christians find themselves between the resurrection and Christ's return. Paul is again encouraging Christians, particularly single Christians, to live with the end in view. All classes of people should keep in mind the impermanence of life.
v 28: Although marriage is certainly not sin, it is troublesome!

11. APPLY: What does society see as the advantages and disadvantages of singleness? Broadly speaking, the benefit of singleness is often seen as the freedom to have sex with who you choose, and as freedom from commitment. But equally, western culture often suggests that there is something wrong with being single: that to be happy and know you are valued, you need to be with someone (though not necessarily married to them).

- **How is this the same and/or different to how the Bible sees it?** The Bible sees the advantage of singleness not in terms of being able to be sexually immoral, but being able to serve God free from other considerations. And, as 1 Corinthians 7 has shown, being single is not an inferior status: it is a gift from God (v 7), and what matters most is having been called by God into relationship with Him (v 17).

12. APPLY: Imagine you have a Christian friend who is married to someone who isn't a Christian. Their faith has caused problems in their marriage, and they're wondering what to do. What advice would you give them, based on 1 Corinthians 7?
Verses 12-14: Persevere in the marriage, even though it's hard. And pray that God would use the relationship to bring the non-Christian spouse to Christ (v 16, see 1 Peter 3 v 1-2).
Verse 15: Don't make your marriage everything: your relationship with God is the most important one you have, and mustn't be sacrificed in order to save the marriage.

- **Imagine you have a Christian friend who is single and would rather not be. How would you encourage them from these verses?**
Verses 8-9, 28: It's good to get married;

there's nothing wrong with hoping one day you'll find a spouse. That said…

Verse 7: Singleness is a God-given gift.

Verse 28: Marriage is actually very hard! It often doesn't seem that way looking in from the outside, and many single Christians feel that they would love to have to cope with the "troubles" of being married. But it's right to remember that having a spouse does not make life easier in every way, and can often make it harder.

Verse 32-35: Singleness enables you to focus entirely on how to please the Lord, rather than needing to consider a spouse. It might be worth asking if such a concern about the Lord's affairs marks them, or are they thinking: "When I find a spouse, then I will serve the Lord". Are they using their singleness well?

7 1 Corinthians 8 – 9
USE YOUR RIGHTS

THE BIG IDEA
Christians are to use their freedoms, and if necessary give up their freedoms and rights, in order to build up other Christians, and bring the gospel message to non-Christians.

SUMMARY
Paul is dealing with the question of whether Christians are free to eat meat sacrificed to idols (8 v 1-6). He makes the point that Christians are free to do this (v 4-6); but immediately encourages Christians who know this not to eat such meat if they are with Christians who think it's sinful (v 7-9, 13). If a Christian's conscience tells them something is sinful, they would be sinning if they do it (even if it is, in fact, not sinful— v 10-12) . And it's the responsibility of a more knowledgeable Christian to give up their freedom to do something in order to help the "weaker" Christian not to sin.

In chapter 9, Paul presents himself as an example: as an apostle, he has the right to be paid, not to have to support himself, and to bring a wife with him (v 4-6). But he does not claim any of these rights (v 15), so that the gospel message can reach as many as possible (v 18). His priority is the spread of the gospel (v 19-23), not enjoying the rights and freedoms that are rightly his as a Christian and as an apostle.

This is a long study. You may want to split it into two sessions, after Q8.

GUIDANCE TO QUESTIONS
1. What are your most important rights? Would you ever give them up? Western culture has at its foundation the notion of rights, which everyone should have, and everyone should enjoy. The right to say what we want; live where we want; believe what we want; marry who we want; be happy; have a family; earn and spend our own money; be safe; have, use and enjoy possessions; and many more.

There is no right answer to the second part of the question. Some people consider it their right never to give up any of their rights! Others may think of situations where they would give up a right: eg: they would give up their right to be safe in order to rescue a child from danger; they would give up their right to say what they want in order not to offend others.

⊻

• **Why are rights so important to us?**

2. Why do we need love as well as knowledge (v 1)? Because to know God is to love Him, too. Knowledge of God always brings with it humility rather than pride. It's only if we love others in the church that we'll exercise our knowledge in the right context, and use it to help others rather than to look or feel good. Knowledge alone will make us feel good about ourselves; knowledge with love will make us want to use it to build others up.

3. What do Christians know about God (v 4, 6)? There is only one real God (v 4, see Deuteronomy 6 v 4). And this one true God is the Creator (v 6); and He is made known through Jesus Christ, who is also our Creator. It's worth noticing that Paul is clearly teaching that Jesus is God here: he describes Him in the same terms as the "one God, the Father".

• **What does this mean about other gods that people worship (v 5-6)?** They are false. Paul acknowledges the claims that many believe that there are other gods. The truth is that there is only one God.

4. What does Paul therefore say all Christians should *know* (v 8)? Food itself is spiritually neutral. We already know God, through Christ (v 6), and we know that God made everything (v 6). Eating meat, whether or not it's been sacrificed to false gods,

makes us no better or worse.

• **So, does it matter whether or not Christians eat meat that has been used in idol worship?** No! (One application for us today is that halal meat is not out of bounds for a Christian to eat.)

Note: Why is this of no importance in the New Testament, when proscribed foods were part of God's law in the Old Testament? The food laws were part of the way God told His people to show that they were distinct from those around them, committed to living differently for Him. But they were only ever external pointers, and unable to change anyone's heart (see Hebrews 7 v 19). Since Jesus came, what matters is making Him King in our hearts, and what sets God's people apart now is not what they eat, but lives lived in obedience to Jesus, acknowledging Jesus as Lord even when pressured not to. So Jesus Himself declared that a person's heart is what matters, and that food laws could not change the inside of a person—and so said that all food is now "clean" (Mark 7 v 14-23).

5. [But some Christians don't know this.] What's the problem if they eat such meat (v 7, 10-11)? Those who see the food as defiled believe it's sinful to eat it because it's been sacrificed to idols, so for them it is sinful. The food becomes defiled not because of the idol, but because of how the food is viewed. It is a dangerous thing to go against conscience; to do something that you consider sinful (even if it isn't). If a Christian thinks something is wrong before God, they shouldn't do it.

6. What point is Paul trying to make to Christians who know it's fine to eat this meat (v 9, 13)? Through a believer eating sacrificed meat because he knows it doesn't matter, a weak brother might be emboldened to do something that he understands as sinful. So the knowledge the first believer has might hurt a weak brother, as he sins against his own conscience.

- **What is the *loving* thing for *knowledgeable* Christians to do?** To not eat this meat, even though they know it isn't wrong—because other Christians think it is wrong, and might copy their example and do something they consider sinful.

- **What point does Paul make in v 12?** To not give up your Christian freedom, when that would help a Christian brother or sister not to sin, is itself sinful. To show how seriously this must be taken, Paul says that to sin against one's brothers in this way is to sin against Christ.

7. APPLY: What principle is Paul establishing as he talks about whether to eat meat sacrificed to idols? We must consider the effects of our actions on other Christians, and give up our rights for the good of others. The priority shouldn't be enjoying the freedom we know we have, but doing whatever is best for our Christian family. Sometimes that will involve not doing something we know we're free to do, so that we don't trip up a Christian friend. We need to see we were not made to care primarily about ourselves.

8. APPLY: …What should Simon be asking himself after talking to Warren?
- Is Warren right about it being sin to buy this new car?
- Is my conscience settled in this decision; should I speak to another Christian to find out what they think?
- If I decide this is a matter of Christian

freedom, I must make sure I don't encourage Warren to buy a new car for himself, because that would be leading him to do something he considers sinful (v 7, 10-11).

- Would it in fact be best not to buy the car—not because it's wrong, but because it might make Warren want to do something his conscience says is wrong?
- When all this is in the past, is there a way I can chat with Warren about why he thinks it's wrong, and not a matter of Christian freedom, to help him see that as Christians we are free to spend our money as we wish, and not make rules about it? **Note:** All Christians should be giving sacrificially (see 2 Corinthians 8 v 1-9), but it is of course possible to buy a new car *and* be giving sacrificially!

- **What should Warren be asking himself after talking to Simon?**
  - Am I right on this, or is my conscience weak?
  - Is buying this new car actually sinful for Simon, or is this an area of Christian freedom?
  - If it is, I need to be humble enough to tell Simon I was mistaken.

- **In what other situations today do Christians need to be careful that our freedom "does not become a stumbling block"?** Examples include: drinking alcohol; the way we speak; constructive criticism around those who find it hard not to grumble; how I dress and speak (thinking of the opposite sex).

If you want to break this session into two, this would be a good place.

9. What does Paul say he is free to do as an apostle? • v 4: To expect those he's working for to feed him

- **v 5:** To have a wife who's also supported by others
- **v 9-12, 14:** To demand to be paid enough to be able to live on for preaching the gospel (ie: to be able to have gospel-proclamation as a full-time, paid job)

10. What has Paul decided to do with the rights he enjoys as a Christian and as an apostle (v 12, 15, 19)? He's forfeited them. He has a right to support, but he hasn't availed himself of it.

- **Why (v 19-22)?** Because he wants to do whatever will further the gospel and build the church. Paul does *whatever* he can, regardless of his rights, to win *whoever* he can. He could earn money for preaching the gospel, but he does it for free. He is free to live without following Jewish customs, but he gives up that freedom so he can win the Jews (v 20). He allows himself to be weak to get alongside weak people (v 22). Because the gospel will reach further, faster, if he doesn't insist on the freedoms and rights he could enjoy as a Christian and apostle, Paul gives it all up.

11. Think back over what you've seen this Corinthian church was like from chapters 1-9. What were their priorities?

⊗

- **You might want to point your group to some or all of these verses:**
  1 v 11-12; 3 v 3-4; 4 v 6; 5 v 1, 12-13; 5 v 2, 6; 7 v 29-32; 8 v 2-9.

- Proving that their particular leader was the best
- Doing what they wanted with their bodies.
- Being tolerant of what other church members chose to do
- Worrying about and trying to change their circumstances (the underlying issue in ch 7)

- Enjoying everything they were free to do.
- **How would verse 19 have been a real challenge to them?** Because Paul sets them an example of doing whatever they can, regardless of their rights, to win whoever they can. Paul's priority is to win people to Christ. Enjoying all that they're free to do, and ensuring they maintain the rights that they have as Christians and as citizens of Corinth, are not to be their motivations for how they live. Instead, they should give up any freedom or right if it will help bring the gospel to someone (9 v 19-23) or help build up a fellow Christian (8 v 9-13).

EXPLORE MORE
What does this look like for him (v 27)? He makes sure that he himself is obeying God in how he uses his body (this might be a reminder to the Corinthian church about their own struggles with sexual immorality, as we saw back in chapters 5 – 6).
How does this encourage any Christians who teach others? And what's the warning? We do not run or fight to no purpose. The prize that we teach about is the prize that we are headed for. But this is a huge warning, too: it is possible for our preaching to save others, but for we ourselves to "be disqualified" by not continuing to live with Christ as Lord ourselves. We are saved by following Christ Jesus as Lord, not by teaching others about Him.

12. APPLY: What rights to we find hardest to be willing to give up? Refer back to Q1 and the rights your group said were most important, or wouldn't be willing to give up. The Getting Personal box below in the Study Guide has some suggestions.

- **How will verses 9 and 19 motivate us to give up the freedoms we hold most dear?** The gospel gives us great freedom, and the "right to become children of God" (John 1 v 12). But the gospel also motivates us to give up our freedom, and hold lightly to all our rights, when:
  - we can keep our Christian brothers and sisters going in the gospel, since that is more important than anything else.
  - we can reach non-Christians with the gospel, since they may be won for Christ, which is more important than anything. In other words, if we understand that the way we live can help people continue as Christians, and become Christians, then we will live in the way which does that, rather than living to enjoy our freedoms and rights.

⊻

- **What does 6 v 9-11 remind us about why the gospel news about the Lord Jesus Christ is absolutely brilliant?** We deserve to be shut out from the kingdom of God; instead, through Christ we have been washed clean, made pure, and found innocent before God, so we can look forward to eternal life.
- **So, how does the brilliance of the gospel message motivate us to give up our freedoms?** Because if by doing so we can help Christians keep trusting in Christ, or help people hear about Christ, then it's well worth giving anything for!

OPTIONAL EXTRA

At the end of this study, and the end of this Good Book Guide, ask your group to think back to the challenges Paul has posed to the Corinthian church in chapters 1 – 9. Ask:
- Which of these is the greatest challenge for your church at the moment?
- How can you individually help your Christian community to face that challenge in a way which helps Christians keep going and growing, and helps non-Christians see and hear the gospel?

Then think together of the truths about God about which Paul has reminded the Corinthian church in chapters 1 – 9. Ask:
- Which has most excited you? Why?

IX 9Marks   Is your church healthy?

9Marks wants to help churches grow in these nine marks of health:

1. Expositional Preaching
2. Biblical Theology
3. A Biblical Understanding of the Gospel
4. A Biblical Understanding of Conversion
5. A Biblical Understanding of Evangelism
6. Biblical Church Membership
7. Biblical Church Discipline
8. Biblical Discipleship
9. Biblical Church Leadership

Find all our titles and other resources at www.9Marks.org.
9Marks exists to equip church leaders with a biblical vision and practical resources for displaying God's glory to the nations through healthy churches.

Best-selling
Good Book Guides

Ezekiel: The God of glory

Tim Chester
Pastor of The Crowded House, Sheffield, UK

"Then they will know that I am the LORD" is the repeated message of Ezekiel. In a world of false hopes that will ultimately fail, this is a message for everyone.

Jonah: The depths of grace

Stephen Witmer
Pastor of Pepperell Christian Fellowship, MA, USA

The book of Jonah reveals to us the depths of God's grace, both to "outsiders" and to "insiders". It shows us God's compassion for the lost and His patience with His wayward people.

Women of faith

Mary Davis
Women's Ministry Director, St Nicholas Church, Tooting, UK

Examine the lives and experiences of seven women from ancient Israel; their flaws, faith, struggles and solutions..

Ephesians: God's big plan for Christ's new people

Thabiti Anyabwile
Senior Pastor, First Baptist Church, Grand Cayman

"If we would be healthy Christians, we would be wise to build our lives around the kind of church that emerges from the book of Ephesians."

Colossians: Confident Christianity

Mark Meynell
Senior Associate Minister, All Souls Church, London, UK

Only if we are convinced about the true identity of Christ, and certain that He alone is all we need to grow, will we mature into confident Christians.

Hebrews: Consider Jesus

Justin Buzzard
Pastor of Garden City Church, San Jose, CA, USA

The letter to the Hebrews helps us leave behind our limited views of Jesus by explaining to us the supreme greatness of Christ Himself.

Recommended Resources

Recommended by
Mark Dever

Listen Up
Christopher Ash

A practical guide to listening to sermons.

"We give Listen Up to all of our new members."

Christianity Explained
Michael Bennett

A tried and tested tool for evangelism which is perfect for one-to-one evangelism.

"A superb tool for evangelism which I have personally used now for over 15 years."

Recommended by
Michael Horton

Christianity Explored
Rico Tice and Barry Cooper

Exploring Jesus in the pages of the Gospel of Mark.

"Christianity Explored offers the best resources for personal and group evangelism available. It's pure gold. Anyone interested in the big questions of life will love this material."

Recommended by
R. Albert Mohler

From creation to new creation
Tim Chester

An accessible Bible overview unlocking the storyline of the whole Bible.

Delighting in the Trinity
Tim Chester

A book to take ordinary Christians in to a deeper understanding of the thrilling triune nature of God.

"These two books pack an enormous amount of theological thinking into a remarkable economy of pages. I commend these books as worthy additions to your library."

Recommended by
D.A. Carson

Men of God
Tim Thornborough

Designed to encourage Christian men to live for Christ: in their homes, workplaces, leisure and in their churches.

"It is a pleasure to recommend a book that faithfully reflects so much Scripture and that presents the application of that Scripture in faithful and sensible ways."

thegoodbook
COMPANY

Opening up the Bible

At The Good Book Company, we are dedicated to helping Christians and local churches grow. We believe that God's growth process always starts with hearing clearly what he has said to us through his timeless word— the Bible.

Ever since we opened our doors in 1991, we have been striving to produce resources that honor God in the way the Bible is used. We have grown to become an international provider of user-friendly resources to the Christian community, with believers of all backgrounds and denominations using our Bible studies, books, evangelistic resources, DVD-based courses and training events.

We want to equip ordinary Christians to live for Christ day by day, and churches to grow in their knowledge of God, their love for one another, and the effectiveness of their outreach.

Call us for a discussion of your needs or visit one of our local websites for more information on the resources and services we provide.

North America: www.thegoodbook.com
UK & Europe: www.thegoodbook.co.uk
Australia: www.thegoodbook.com.au
New Zealand: www.thegoodbook.co.nz

North America: 866 244 2165
UK & Europe: 0333 123 0880
Australia: (02) 6100 4211
New Zealand (+64) 3 343 1990

www.christianityexplored.org

Our partner site is a great place for those exploring the Christian faith, with a clear explanation of the good news, powerful testimonies and answers to difficult questions.

One life. What's it all about?